simple
enchanted
beading

CHERYL OWEN

simple enchanted beading

OVER 30 DELIGHTFUL PROJECTS TO CAPTIVATE AND CHARM

D&C

David and Charles

Printed in China by SNP Leefung
for David & Charles
Brunel House   Newton Abbot   Devon

Commissioning Editor Ali Myer
Editor Jennifer Fox-Proverbs
Desk Editor Bethany Dymond
Art Editor Sarah Underhill
Senior Designer Charly Bailey
Designer Lisa Wyman
Project Editor Betsy Hosegood
Production Controller Ros Napper
Photographer Karl Adamsson

Visit our website at
www.davidandcharles.co.uk

David & Charles books are available from all
good bookshops; alternatively you can contact our
Orderline on 0870 9908222 or write to us at FREEPOST
EX2 110, D&C Direct, Newton Abbot, TQ12 4ZZ (no stamp
required UK only); US customers call 800-289-0963 and
Canadian customers call 800-840-5220.

Contents

a world of enchantment

Anyone who has ever dreamed has touched the hidden world of enchantment where magical things can happen, a world of fairies and water nymphs, of angels and sprites. This is also the world of Nature – who could see a kaleidoscope of magnificent butterflies feeding on a field of flowers or a dragonfly hovering over a pond like some prehistoric creature in miniature without believing in the presence of magic?

Nature is both the source and the dwelling place for all enchanted things. It was Nature that first inspired the myths, like the story of Jack Frost, the son of the Norse god of Wind, and it is in Nature's hidden places that magical creatures lurk: the clearings of dark woods where fairies gather to dance between the toadstools, and the bottoms of wells where sprites and other water-dwellers live.

It is difficult to describe these things in words, and even harder to re-create them as art, but with beads things become a whole lot easier. This is because beads already express many of the qualities we so admire in Nature – beauty, intricacy, transparency or translucency, shine and shimmer. Some beads,

made from semi-precious stones, even have magical qualities and are said to bring protection, love, valour or other good things to the wearer.

Once you have found a source of magical beads, your only task is to put them together in the right way to communicate the theme. This is where this book comes in. It contains a wide range of projects – enchanting jewellery (see pages 30, 76, 81, 92, 102 and 110), accessories (pages 40, 44, 60, 64, 70, 82, 98, 106 and 114), and items for the home (pages 34, 50, 55 and 88). Along the way you'll learn some simple and exciting techniques that you can utilize for other beading projects and there are plenty of motifs and templates that you can copy and use for coordinating items.

You don't need any beading experience to make these projects because each one is suitable for beginners and is accompanied by easy-to-follow step-by-step instructions. Many of them make lovely gifts, though you may wish to make them for yourself too. So get started now, give your mystical imagination free rein and have fun indulging in the magical world of beads, sprites and Nature's delights.

the magic of beads

A good bead shop is like Aladdin's cave, packed with twinkling, glittering, colourful things that cry out to be taken home and turned into something beautiful. In fact, as soon as you walk in it will seem as if the magic has begun. Beads can be polished glass, precious or semi-precious stones, exotic woods, pearls, shells, metal, resin, plastics and much, much more. Add to this the amazing variety of bead shapes, including doughnuts, cylinders, spheres, cubes, pyramids, cone-shapes, drops and so on, and you'll start to get the idea of how fantastic the alternatives are. In fact, unless you know what you want before you visit a large bead store or surf the Internet, you'll soon be overwhelmed.

Every project in this book has a precise list of Magical Ingredients that will help you make the right choices. You don't have to buy exactly what is listed, but you should make sure that even if your beads are made out of different materials or come in different colours, they are the same size as the ones listed. This is particularly important for items such as the daisy necklace (page 76) and clematis ring (page 102) because if your beads are different sizes they won't sit together in the way that is planned in the project. The pictures on the following pages should help inspire your purchases.

The size of the beads you choose should reflect the item you are making. Large, bright beads are ideal for the charm bracelet shown opposite, for example, (see page 30), while smaller beads are used for loom work (see page 105 for the bracelet below).

beads to inspire you...

The **spear-shaped beads** here express the shape of the dragonfly's wings better than anything else, while gold rocailles create the body. **Rocailles** are particularly useful beads, ideal for embroidery, and come in a huge range of colours, sizes and finishes. (See page 44 for this project.)

A flat, cranberry coloured **oval bead** is perfect for suggesting an acorn, but what really carry off the effect here are the bands of **cylinder beads** that create the 'cup' (see page 82). Being uniform and regular in shape, cylinder beads sit together tightly, which is why they are also popular for bead weaving. They have large holes, which can be handy too. **Delica** is a brand of cylinder bead.

Crystals add fairytale sparkle to any project, especially the fire-polished stones that flash colours in the light like a darting dragonfly. The one on the end of this snowflake is a **drop bead** or pendant, and these are ideal where you want beads to swing enticingly. (See page 40 for this project).

Bicone beads have tapered ends and cut sides to catch the light. They look rather like the beads you see on expensive rings, especially when made of crystal, so they are great for sparkling jewellery, like this super clematis ring (page 102).

Semi-precious stones are cheaper if you buy chips, and they look great too. They add a touch of luxury to any project, like this lovely brooch (see page 92), and many are believed to have special healing powers, which make them especially appropriate for these project.

Pearls used to be wildly expensive, but now that freshwater pearls can be easily produced and because of the realistic imitation pearls that are also widely available, they are accessible to all. They come in many lovely colours, including the warm cranberry colour used for these berry earrings. (See page 110 for this project.)

Doughnut beads and other special shapes make wonderful focus beads. These striking examples are made from green-dyed mother-of-pearl, and have a lovely natural quality that helps to express the strong link between fairies and woodlands. This project begins on page 34.

Imitation coins, like the ones on the bag shown below (see page 87) remind us of the pot of gold at the end of the rainbow and other lovely myths.

Charms come in many sizes, shapes and designs and a few basic metallic colours. Look out for fairies and anything with a flying or natural theme such as butterflies, dragonflies, flowers, four-leaf clovers and so on. This pretty charm bracelet (see page 30) uses a range of charms with a flying theme, while the beads and ribbon ties have been chosen to suggest the flowers.

words of wisdom...

Use birthstones to personalize your gifts:

January – garnet
February – amethyst
March – aquamarine
April – diamond
May – emerald
June – pearl
July – ruby
August – peridot
September – sapphire
October – opal
November – topaz
December – turquoise

Sequins are inexpensive plastic discs that are flat or cup shaped and come in many sizes, shapes and finishes. Sequins with metallic or sparkling finishes are ideal for adding glamour and enhance a natural or supernatural theme. These gold sequins look great on this belt (see page 98).

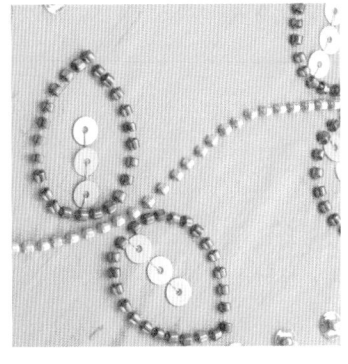

Special shapes, like hearts, butterflies and so on are wonderful focal points that you can build your design around, as on this primrose table setting (see page 88). Use them sparingly for best effect.

fae fabrics and foundations

Now that you have the right projects, the beautiful beads, some appropriate charms and so on, you'll need something to stitch them onto so you can fulfil the fantasy. Basically beads can be attached to anything cloth or paper based or they can be joined to each other with metal to make jewellery (see pages 14–15). The choice of foundation is of key importance because it needs to set the right tone without overpowering the bead embroidery, which is the main feature of the piece. There's no point spending time creating a beautiful bead embroidery if the fabric or paper base is too flimsy or in a clashing colour, pattern or texture.

When using fabric, look for one that is fairly closely woven so that it is strong enough to support the beads. On the whole, natural fabrics are best for the projects in this book, although some synthetics are acceptable if they are dazzling enough. For this reason, cotton, linen and silk are recommended here, especially silks with a sheen such as dupion or taffeta. If you think the fabric is a little thin, apply iron-on interfacing to the back to strengthen it.

When it comes to paper or card items, such as greetings cards and boxes, you have two options. You can either work on fabric and then mount it on the card, as for the magical greetings card on page 56, or you can work directly on card or paper. Japanese handmade papers are ideal here because they are thick enough to hide the threads on the back and luscious enough to link to the ethereal subject matter. Just make sure that you don't work your stitches too close together or you'll find you've cut the paper.

Other items to consider are embellishments, such as ribbons, and threads. Ribbons and braids provide a quick way of finishing a project. Use them to create borders or tie them on to dangle and flutter enticingly. Threads can be either practical or fanciful. For strength use a proper beading thread such as Nymo. Polyester sewing and quilting threads are also used in this book for stitching on beads. When using a sewing thread, run it over beeswax before you begin to strengthen it and help prevent or reduce tangling.

Jade **silk dupion** and a paler **silk taffeta** are combined on this glorious cushion. Not only do these fabrics conjure up the colours of a woody dell, but they have a shiny finish that reminds us of sunlight playing through the tree canopy and of the flash of bright wings. (See page 34 for this project.)

Some wonderful **boucle yarn** is key in creating this fairy's fabulous hair. You only need a scrap, so look out for sample packs that contain small amounts of fancy yarn. That way you can make several fairies, all with different locks. Appropriate fabrics are also important here – **fine cotton** for the body and **organza** for a diaphanous dress all contribute to creating the perfect little princess. (See page 70 to make this fairy.)

With its lovely crisp, evenweave texture, **linen** is a wonderful foil for beadwork. Its subtle appearance allows the beading to take centre stage, but it is also luxurious enough to enhance the finished item. It is ideal for this lavender sachet (see page 49).

Quilting thread was used to weave this enchanting mushroom charm (see page 64) but **Nymo thread** would also be a good choice and is even stronger. Use Nymo thread Size B for square weaving as it is fine enough to allow the needle to pass through the beads many times.

all that glitters

Gold, silver and other metals are strongly linked to the enchanted world. Of course, you don't need to buy solid gold or silver unless you want to, and in fact solid gold can be very soft and delicate so it is best left to the experts. Instead look out for plated items or simply buy the much cheaper metals, such as nickel, which, if carefully chosen, will do the job just as well.

The metal items you are likely to need are mainly for jewellery. If you have sensitive skin you'll need to be careful in your choice but not necessarily for every part of the jewellery. For example, when making earrings the ear wire or ear fitting can be gold or hypo-allergenic metal, while the rest of the earring can be anything you like because it won't touch your skin.

clasps and fittings

Necklaces and bracelets often require clasps. These come in many shapes and sizes and usually in gold or silver colours, though sometimes you can get other metallic shades. Some clasps screw together – and these are usually the most secure – while others involve a simple spring fitting (lobster and spring-ring clasps) or a ring and bar combination (toggle clasp). Earrings need a fitting that attaches to your ear. Fish-hook fittings for pierced ears are the most widely available, but you can also buy posts, hoops and lever-backs (also for pierced ears). If your ears aren't pierced, finding the right fitting is more difficult and choices are limited, but a local jeweller may be able to help.

Thick green **enamelled wire** is the basis for this festive napkin ring, which is then bound with finer wire. The fine wire is beaded and shaped into leaves for a simple but effective table decoration (see page 55).

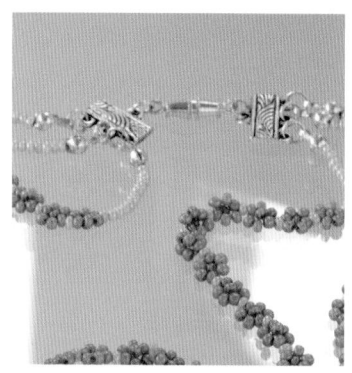

The lovely **torpedo clasp** and three-hole end bars used here enhance the delicacy of this super multi-strand daisy-chain necklace (see page 76). They have been carefully chosen to enhance the style and colours of the necklace and are sized to match.

Why bother with an expensive chain when a beautiful **ribbon** will do just as well for hanging a pendant? This lovely organza ribbon looks wonderful with the berry pendant it is supporting.

metal for attaching beads

To attach beads to each other you can use wire, chain or both. You'll need wire snips to cut these plus chain-nose (flat-nose) and round-nose pliers to manipulate the wire. Wire is available in various thicknesses (gauges) and colours to suit different projects. The materials list with each project will tell you which type to buy. You can also get very useful short lengths of wire that are blocked at one end with a flattened tip like a pin or with a ball or decorative motif on the end. These are called headpins and they are perfect for making dangling strings of beads. See below for instructions on a simple way to use headpins.

using a headpin

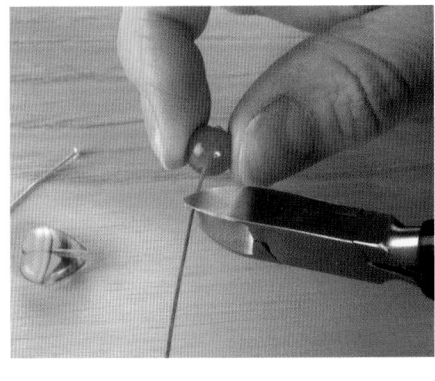

1 Slide your chosen bead(s) onto the headpin. The flattened or decorative end will prevent them sliding off. Push the bead(s) down to the end and use wire snips to cut through the wire about 8mm (5/16in) above the last bead.

2 Using round-nose pliers, bend the wire above the bead into a loop so that it meets the wire emerging from the bead. Make sure the end touches the wire above the bead.

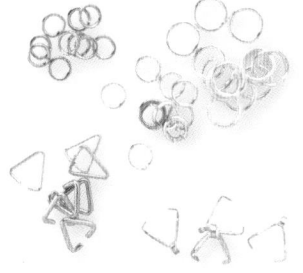

using jump rings

Jump rings are excellent for joining jewellery components together. Open the jump ring by grasping it on each side of the join and twisting in opposite directions. This ensures that after you have slipped on the components you can close the jump ring into a circle. If you pull the ring open outwards, once it is closed it will look slightly distorted and it is more liable to break.

timeless techniques

The beadwork in this book is all fairly simply and straightforward, utilizing stitches you may well know from dressmaking or embroidery, but there may be a few techniques that are new to you, and you'll find all the information you need to help you right here and in the projects which follow.

The beads can either be attached to fabric or to each other and to findings. Attaching the beads to fabric is fairly straightforward, and you'll find instructions for this on the next few pages. Joining beads to each other, either to make fabulous fringing or to create a dense fabric of beads is a little more challenging, but you should have no problems if you work through the instructions on pages 20–26, and just think what you'll be able to achieve once you've learnt the techniques.

Coppery cylindrical beads applied to the top of this bag and on both edges of the handle add an elegant touch. These beads are applied as **single beads**.

getting started

Make sure your fabric is smooth and clean – iron it if necessary. In order to prevent puckering you should mount the fabric in an embroidery frame or hoop before you begin stitching, just as if you were doing ordinary embroidery. The fabric should be at least 5cm (2in) larger than the hoop. Trace the design onto the fabric (see page 122) before mounting it in the hoop. Now you are ready to begin.

adding single beads

Sometimes you may wish to add single beads, perhaps as a feature on a motif or as a scattering over a large item, such as a cushion.

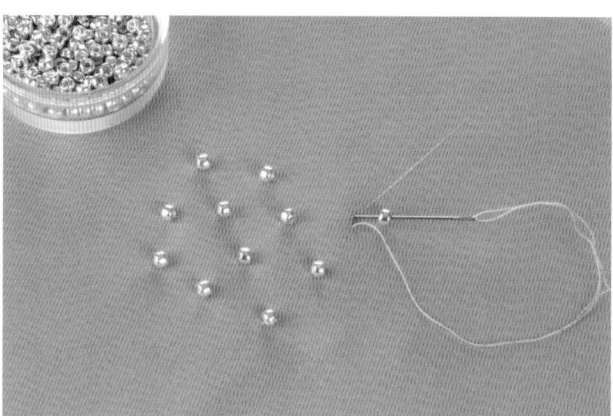

To sew on a single bead, bring the needle to the right side and thread on the bead. Insert the needle to the back of the fabric at the other side of the bead. Repeat to secure the bead.

Working in backstitch, lines of beads can be added to any item, here creating some of the veins on a butterfly's wings. (See page 60 for instructions on making this butterfly, and page 18 for information on applying lines of beads using a backstitch technique.)

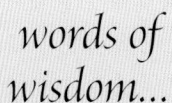

Attaching a sequin with a bead creates a professional look. The thread becomes more or less invisible, especially if you choose a thread colour that matches the bead. Instructions on making this fairy are on page 75 and details on attaching a sequin with a bead are on page 18.

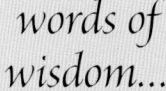

Attaching a sequin without a bead, can create a subtle, elegant look, as on the leaf veins of this exquisite belt. (See page 98 for details on making this belt and page 19 for information on attaching a sequin without a bead.)

Using a bead loom, explained in detail on pages 24–26, makes producing a decorative beaded band really straightforward. Bands are ideal for a bracelet or simply as a decorative embellishment, as on this lovely box (see page 106).

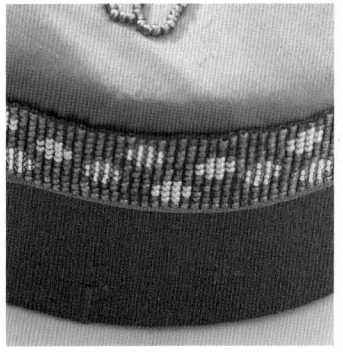

Square stitch (see page 22) enables you to make lovely freeform beaded shapes, like this simple mushroom design, which makes an unusual handbag charm (see page 64).

17

working in backstitch

Backstitch is ideal for stitching a row of beads as when outlining a motif.
Use Delica (cylinder) beads or small rocailles to outline intricate shapes.

1 Knot your thread. Bring the needle to the right side and thread on beads – pick up one or two beads to follow a curved line but as many as four beads on a straight line. Lay the beads end to end on the fabric and insert the needle into the fabric after the last bead.

2 Bring the needle to the right side between the last and second from last bead. Insert the needle through the last bead and then pick up more beads to continue as in step 1. With a little practice you will find the process quick and easy.

attaching a sequin with a bead

Fixing a sequin to fabric with a bead on top is a practical method and adds an extra decorative touch. The bead can be the same colour as the sequin or a contrasting colour. Use thread that matches the colour of the bead.

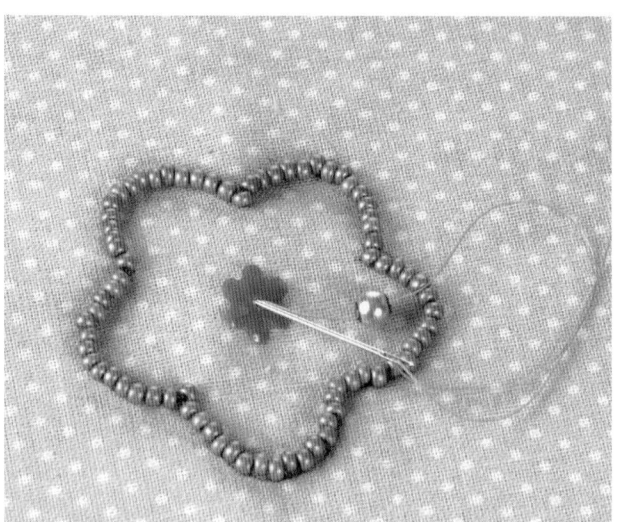

1 Knot your thread. Bring the needle to the right side of the fabric and thread on a sequin and then a bead. The bead should be smaller than the sequin.

2 Insert the needle back through the sequin and the fabric, as shown. Pull the thread so that the bead sits on top of the sequin like the centre of a flower.

attaching a sequin without a bead

Sometimes you don't want to have a bead on top of the sequin. In this case attach it as explained here.

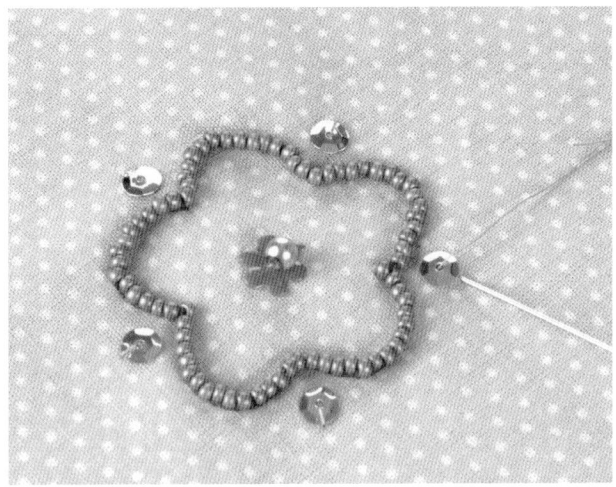

Bring the needle to the right side and thread on the sequin. Now insert the needle into the fabric at one side of the sequin, as shown. Secure the thread ends on the back of the fabric.

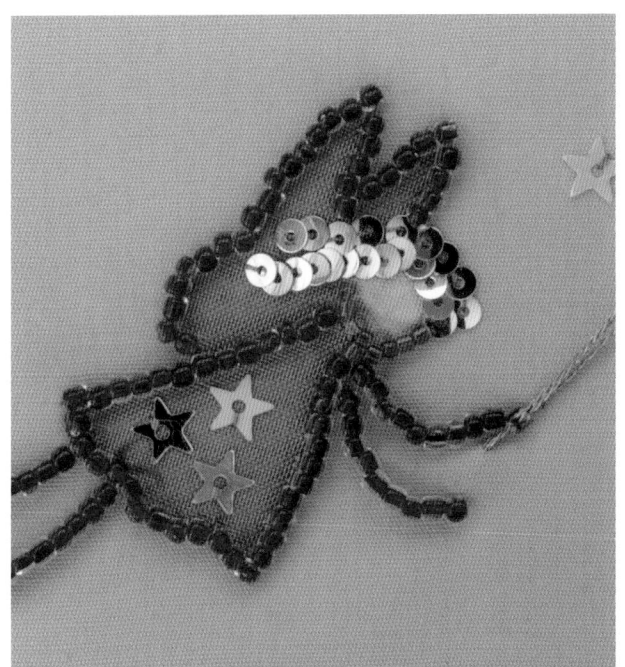

Overlapping sequins

If you wish to create a strong, solid line of sequins you can overlap them, as explained here. Use a thread that matches the sequins rather than the fabric.

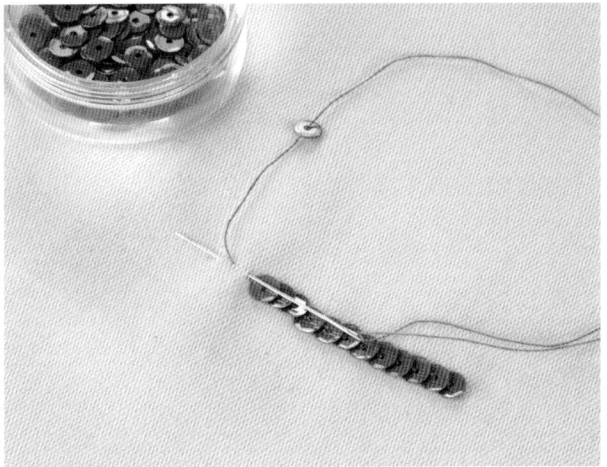

Bring the needle to the right side and thread on one sequin. Insert the needle to the wrong side at the sequin's edge, as when working backstitch. Now bring the needle to the right side half a sequin's width away, thread on the sequin and insert the needle through the fabric at the edge of the previous sequin. Continue adding sequins in this way with a backstitch.

The fairy on this lovely greetings card (see page 56) is an excellent example of how you might attach sequins without a bead. The stars on her dress have been attached individually as explained above left, while the round sequins for her hair are attached in an overlapping line as explained above right. In this case the thread used matches the pink of the fairy's wings and dress to emphasize the colour theme.

frolicking fringing

Give a project added movement with a beaded fringe. It will catch the light and move as sensuously as a water nymph trying to catch the eye of a passing knight. It's not difficult to do and you can create a remarkable number of different patterns. The easiest of these are simple stranded fringes, like the one illustrated here. Once you have mastered the basics you can create a looped fringe or try netting (see opposite).

The pearl fringe around this delightful evening bag is basically a standard fringe except that a line of small pearls were attached around the bag opening before the fringing was added. Notice the large drop bead at the lower end of each fringed strand. These beads add weight and catch the eye. For further details on making this fringe, see page 87.

making a stranded fringe

1 Lay out the fabric on a flat surface and mark the position of each strand with a pin. Thread a beading needle with a long length of strong thread, such as Nymo. Secure the thread to the corner of the piece (or first pin mark if you are working on a circular item). Thread on beads until the fringe is the required length then thread a small bead on the end to act as a permanent stop bead.

2 Insert the needle back through all the beads except the stop bead. Pull the thread so that the beads sit end to end. Make a small stitch in the edge of the fabric above the fringe to secure the strand and continue on to the next pin mark. Once you have finished the fringing, knot the thread securely and darn in the end.

words of wisdom...

If you are working on a single thickness of fabric, as on a scarf, work tiny running stitches along the edge between each strand of the fringe. If the edge of the fabric is double, insert the needle between the layers of fabric and bring it out at the next pin mark.

nifty netting

Netting is similar to fringing but it is worked in a different way to create an open, lacy look. It can be added to the hem or edge of a scarf, mat or cushion, for example, or can stand alone as a lovely piece of jewellery or a napkin ring. The instructions below show you how to bead a ready-made scarf, but the principle is the same on any item.

words of wisdom...

To decide on your bead order, thread beads onto a length of thread without knotting the end and lift both ends of thread to form a loop. Check the effect and rearrange the beads until you are happy with the design. Use this as your beading guide.

netting a scarf

1 Lay the fabric out flat. Mark the position of each loop of the top row with a pin. Thread a beading needle with a long length of thread, preferably strong beading thread. Secure the thread to the corner of the fabric. Thread on beads for the first loop. There should be an uneven number of beads and a feature bead at the centre. Make a small stitch in the edge of the fabric at the first pin mark. Insert the needle back through the last bead, as shown.

2 Thread on beads for the next loop in the same order as before. Make a small stitch in the edge of the fabric at the next pin as before and continue making loops between the pin marks until you reach the end.

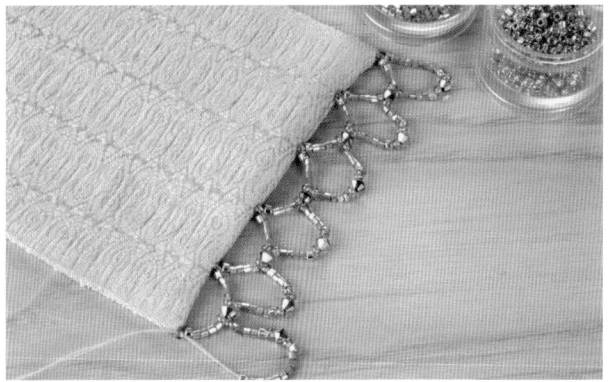

3 Insert the needle through the last bead on the row. Thread on beads for the first loop of the second row: you will need to add more beads on the outer half of the loop so that the feature bead hangs centrally. Hold up the fabric to see how the loop hangs. Insert the needle through the middle bead on the last loop of the first row.

4 Continue making the second row by inserting the needle through the middle bead of the adjacent loop above and threading beads to match the inner half of the first loop of the second row. Make the last loop longer on the outside edge as you did for the first loop on that row. Secure the thread to the fabric or add another row.

needleweaving for nymphs

Sometimes you'll want to create an item out of beads alone, without stitching them to a base fabric, and you can do this by weaving them together. The basic stitch is known as square stitch, and this is used to make the toadstool handbag charms (page 64) and pendant, right. Needleweaving can also be used in place of loom weaving. It will take longer on a large project but it is more durable because the needle passes through the beads more often.

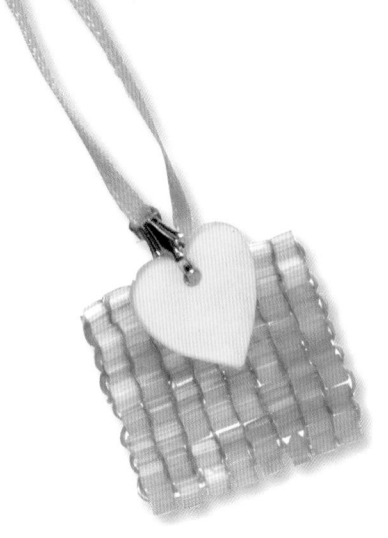

working square stitch

1 Use a contrasting bead as a stop bead so you won't get confused into thinking it is part of the design. Thread a stop bead onto the thread then insert the needle through the bead again once or twice, leaving a trailing end of thread about 20cm (8in) long.

2 Thread on the required number of beads for the first row. Thread on another bead, which will be the first bead of the second row (here shown in blue). Insert the needle through the last bead of the first row, as shown.

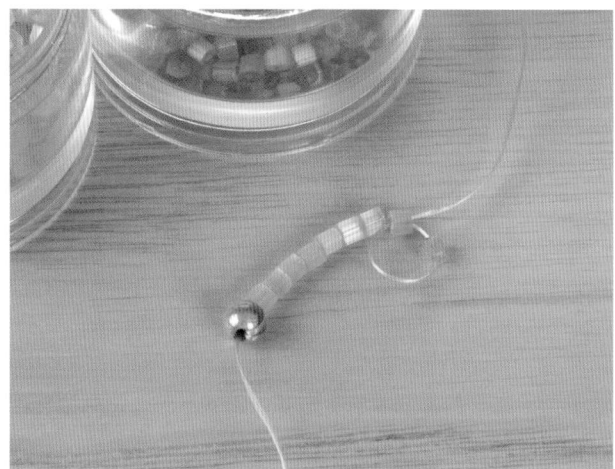

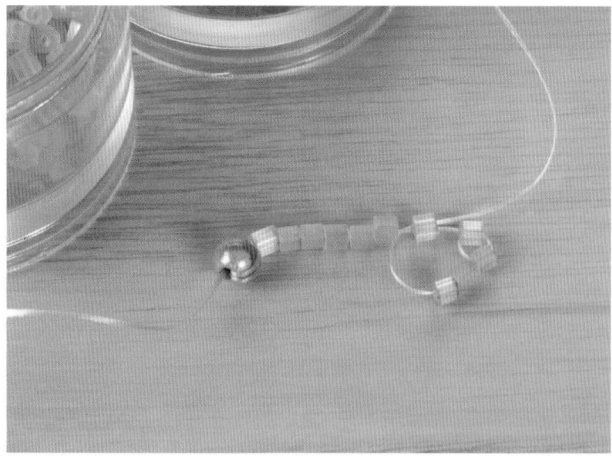

3 Turn the needle and insert it through the first bead of the second row again, as shown.

4 Thread on the next bead and insert the needle through the second from last bead on the first row.

5 Turn the needle and insert it through the bead just added. Now thread on the next bead and continue in the same way until you reach the end of the row.

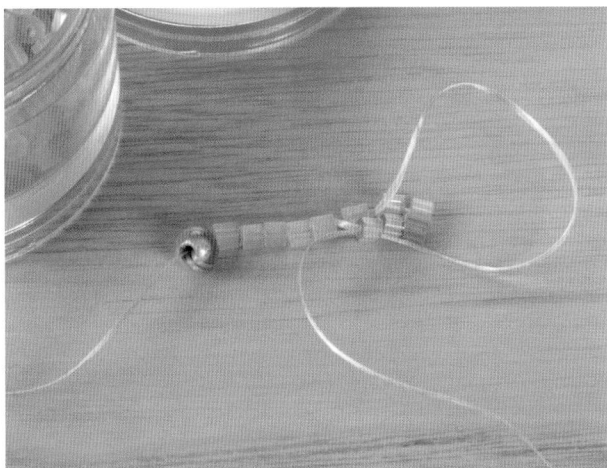

6 At the end of the row, insert the needle through the whole first row of beads.

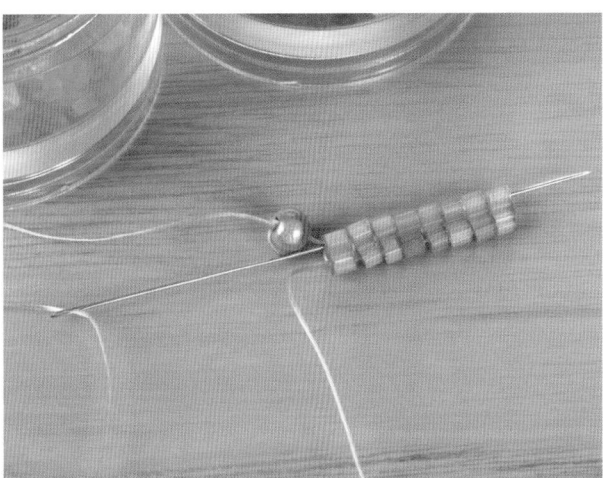

7 Turn the needle and return it through the entire second row. Continue working rows in this way until you have reached the required depth.

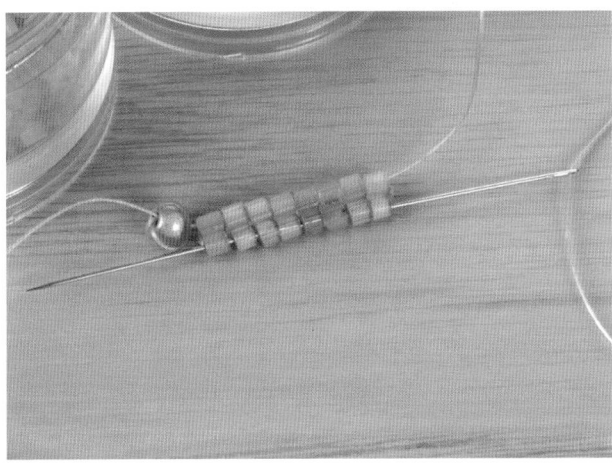

8 To finish, weave the thread through the previous two rows then cut off the excess thread. Remove the stop bead at the beginning and then work the trailing end into the woven beads.

words of wisdom...

If you run out of thread, weave it through the previous rows. To start a new thread, weave the thread through the previous two rows and thread on a bead to begin beading again at the place where you ran out. Secure the finishing knot with a dab of beading glue or clear nail varnish.

winning weaves

If you wish to create a solid strip of beads, the easiest and quickest way to do so is on a bead loom. Basic looms can make bands up to 6cm (2½in) wide, which can be made into pretty bracelets and chokers or used to trim boxes (see page 106) and soft furnishings.

    With a bead loom you can create some quite intricate designs, even producing pictures or words in beads. You'll need a plan to follow for this, and graph paper is ideal here, enabling you to create a coloured chart to work from.

Size 9 rocaille beads are the most versatile size for bead weaving, though Delica beads and cylinder beads also work well because they are uniform in size. Ideally use a strong beading thread such as Nymo, though you can also use sewing or quilting thread if you run it over some beeswax to harden it first.

This simple bead loom is all you need to get started.

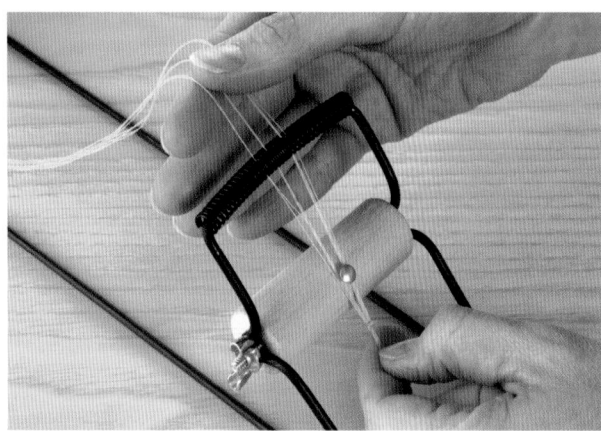

using a bead loom

1 Cut the warp threads, which will lay lengthwise in the loom, 50cm (20in) longer than the intended finished length of the beading. Each bead will sit between two warp threads, so cut one more warp thread than the number of beads across a row. Tie the threads together with a knot at one end and divide the bundle of threads in two. Slip the knot under the nail head on one of the wooden rollers.

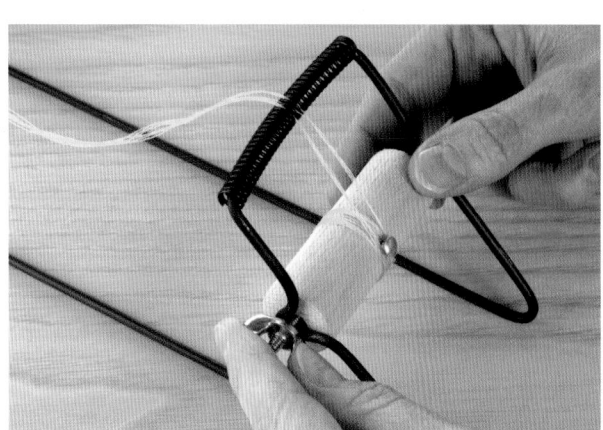

2 Hold the threads taut and turn the roller to wind the warp threads until there is just enough thread left to tie around the other roller. Tighten the wing nut to hold the roller in place.

This super bracelet is worked using a bead loom like the one shown here.

3 Position the threads in the grooves of the metal spring, using a needle to separate the threads. Turn the loom so that the roller and metal spring you have been working on is furthest from you. Now position the threads in the grooves of the metal spring that is nearest to you, holding the threads taut.

4 Tie the threads under the nail of the roller that is nearest to you. Turn the roller to tighten the threads then tighten the wing nut, as you did at the other end. Now you are ready to begin beading.

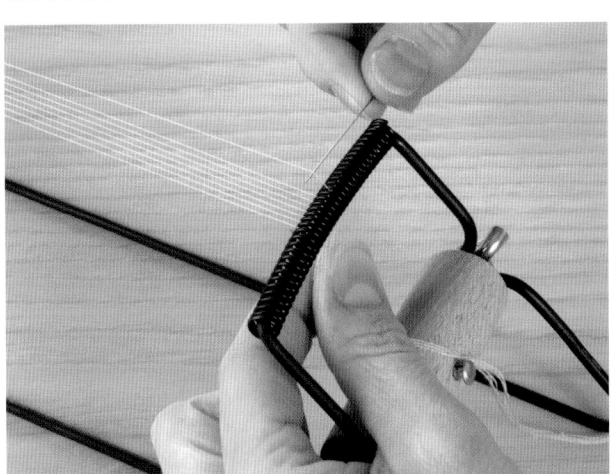

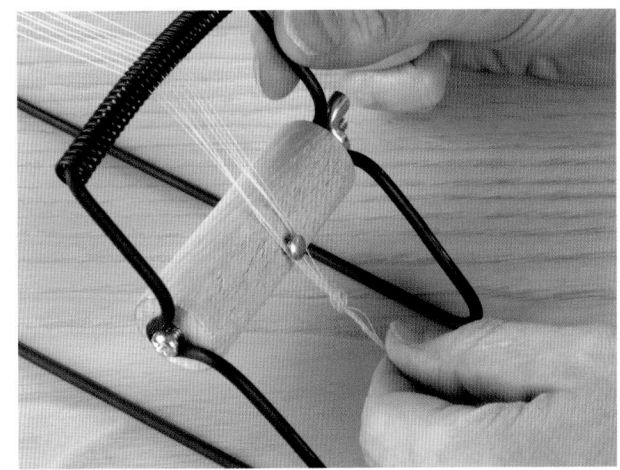

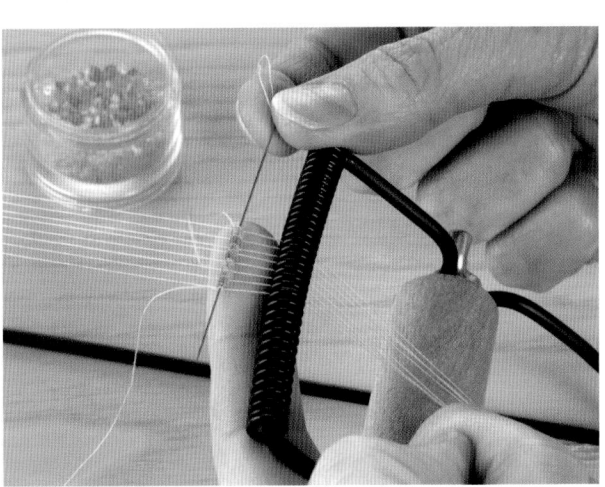

5 Thread a long length of thread for the weft thread onto the beading needle. Tie the thread to an outside thread close to the roller nearest you, leaving a 15cm (6in) trailing end of thread. Thread on the required number of beads for one row and slip them down the working thread. Position the threads at right angles under the warp threads then press them up between the warp threads with a finger.

6 Insert the needle back through the beads, making sure that the needle passes above the warp threads. Because the thread in step 5 went below the warp threads and this strand runs above the warp thread, the beads are firmly held in place.

7 Pick up the next row of beads and repeat the process. Push the rows of beads together as you work to keep the weaving neat and uniform. When you run out of thread, weave in a new piece as explained in the tip on page 23. Loosen the tension on the rollers when you need to use the extra length of threads and roll the beadwork onto the roller at the start.

8 When the beadwork is the desired length, loosen the tension on the rollers and lift off the work. Cut off the knots. Work the extending threads back into the work by threading them on a needle through the beads. If you wish to add a bead and loop fastening, leave two threads at the centre of the ends of the beadwork. Cut off the excess threads.

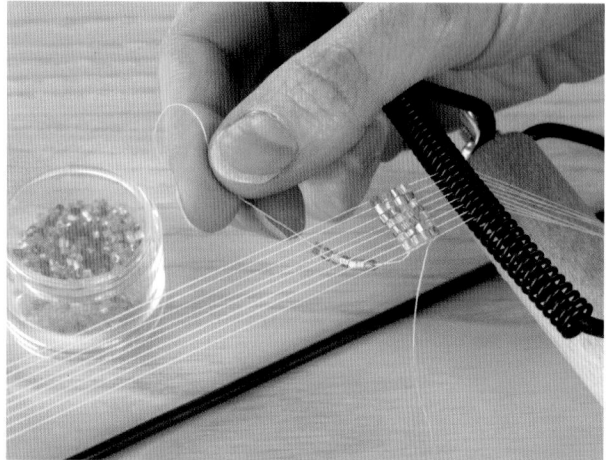

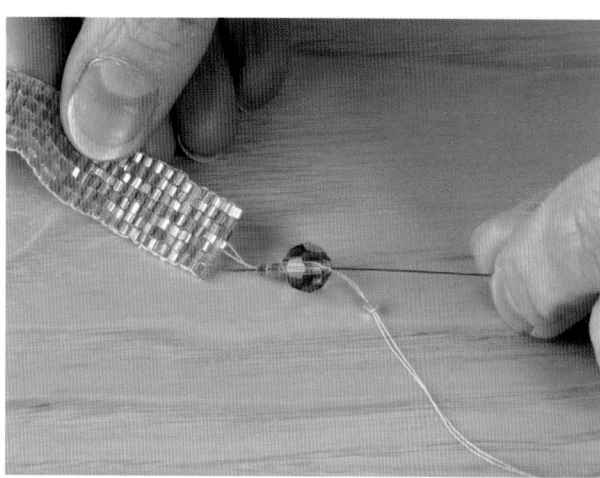

9 To make a clasp, at one end of the weaving, thread both threads onto a needle and thread on two small beads to match those used for the weaving, thread on one large bead and another small bead. Insert the needle back through all the beads except the last one. Tie the threads around an outer weft thread then weave the threads back into the work. Cut off the excess thread.

10 At the other end of the weaving, thread two small beads onto both threads. Thread on enough small beads to make a loop to slip over the large bead at the opposite end of the bracelet. Insert the needle through the two small beads. Tie the threads around an outer weft thread then weave the threads back into the work. Cut off the excess thread.

words of wisdom...

If you'd like to weave a design into your piece but aren't sure where to start, take a look at some cross-stitch or knitting patterns. A cross-stitch border design works wonderfully as a beaded band.

words of wisdom...

Always use beads that are the same size. If you pick up a larger or smaller bead, don't use it because it will make your work uneven. Likewise, discard any beads that are uneven, cracked or that the needle won't pass easily through.

This charming clematis bracelet features both needleweaving and loom weaving. The flower is woven by hand while the band it adorns is made using a loom. For further details of this project see page 105.

the projects

In today's noisy concrete world it's good to take time out, to get off the treadmill and to try to reconnect with nature and the old ways. Let the projects in this book distract you from daily worries and from the grind of repetitive tasks and instead envelop you in their colours and light, bright theme. Let them infuse you with magic and fill you with mischievous imagination. Put on the daisy necklace (page 76) and feel inspired to dance barefoot through a forest, slip the toadstool charm on your bag (page 64) and skip impishly along the corridors or make a cushion inspired by a fairy ring (page 34) and let it take you to another world.

Of course, the projects in this book aren't just for you. They are ideal for little girls and for big girls who are little girls at heart. So set free your inner fairy godmother and make a tooth fairy box for a small relative (page 44), send a card to a friend just to let them know you've been thinking of them (page 56) or make a scarf for the fairy godmother in your own life (page 114). You'll find there are plenty of projects here for you to choose from, nearly all of which can be completed in only a few hours – all you need is an evening or an afternoon to spare.

charm bracelet

Silk ribbon, floral beads and silver charms capture the colours and delights of a summer garden or fairy dell on this deceptively easy-to-make bracelet. Have fun hunting out suitable charms, floral and leafy beads and ribbon in toning colours to make a bracelet that is both mystical and gorgeous. Wear it to remind you of life and growth throughout the year.

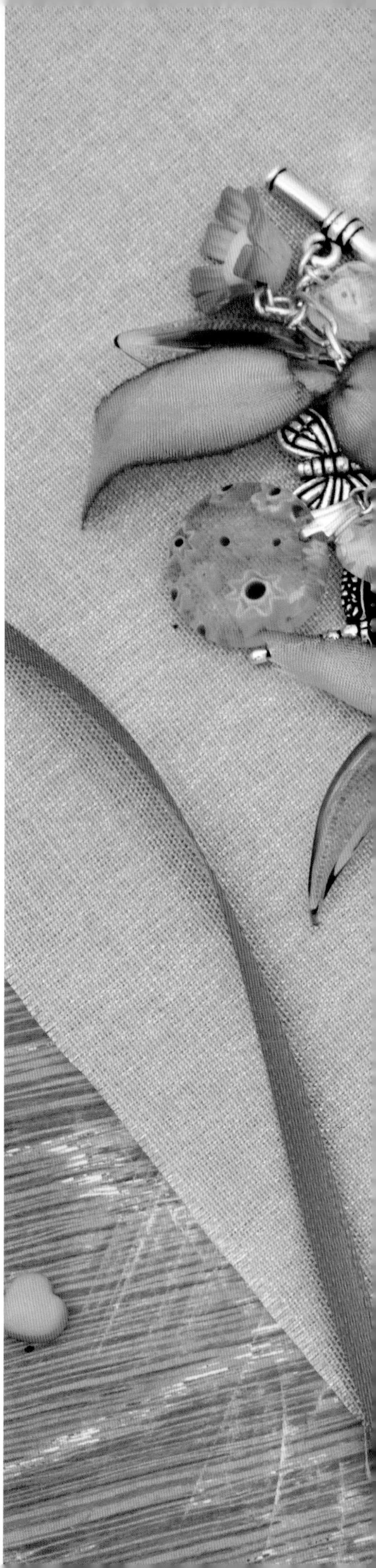

This beautiful bracelet is embellished with silk bias ribbon in sunset colours. Look out for similar ribbon or combine plain ribbons in toning hues.

the magic ingredients...

about 20 assorted beads and pendants in the colours of the garden, including some leaf or flower shapes

4 silver charms

32cm (12½in) of 1cm (³/₈in) wide pink and yellow shaded silk bias ribbon

20cm (8in) silver chain

26 x 4mm (¹/₈in) silver jump rings

up to 20 x 2.5cm (1in) silver headpins (for the beads)

1.2cm (½in) toggle necklace fastening

round-nose pliers

 wire snips

words of wisdom...

Dab the joins of the jump rings with instant-bonding glue for extra security.

1 Open a jump ring by twisting it sideways using two pairs of pliers or your round-nose pliers and the finger and thumb of your free hand. Slip it onto the end of the chain. Slip the ring of a toggle necklace fastening onto the jump ring as well then close the jump ring tightly.

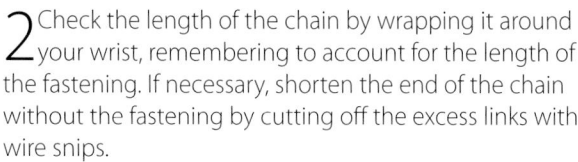

2 Check the length of the chain by wrapping it around your wrist, remembering to account for the length of the fastening. If necessary, shorten the end of the chain without the fastening by cutting off the excess links with wire snips.

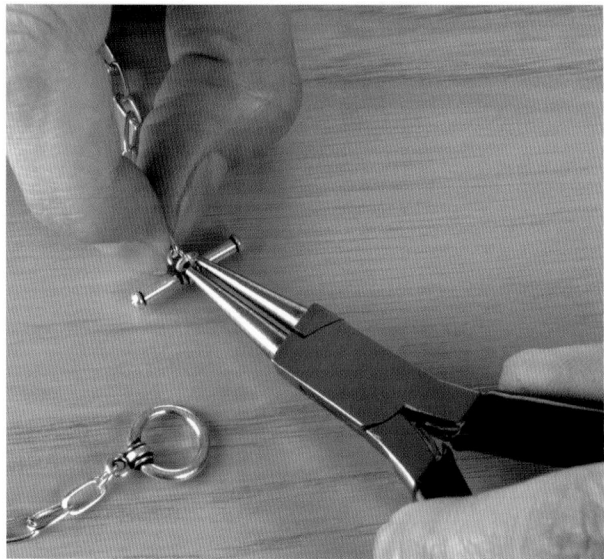

3 Open a jump ring and slip it onto the free end of the chain. Slip the bar of the necklace fastening onto the jump ring. Close the jump ring, as before, using the round-nose pliers.

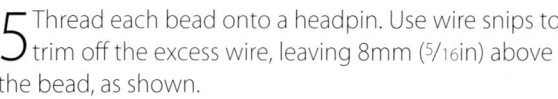

4 Cut the ribbon into four 8cm (3⅛in) lengths. Spacing the ribbon lengths equally along the chain, tie each one to a link. Trim the ribbon ends diagonally.

5 Thread each bead onto a headpin. Use wire snips to trim off the excess wire, leaving 8mm (5⁄16in) above the bead, as shown.

6 Hold each headpin with the round-nose pliers 3mm (⅛in) from the tip and bend the wire into a loop around the pliers, moving the wire towards you as you form the loop so that it is centred over the bead.

7 Lay out the beads, pendants and charms beside the chain in a pleasing arrangement of shapes and colours. Fix each piece onto the lower edge of each link of the chain except those tied with ribbon by slipping a jump ring onto the ring of each piece then onto the chain. Close the jump rings tightly.

fairy-ring cushion

Inspired by fairy rings, this 30cm (12in) square cushion will bring an elfin look to a bedroom or living room. In folklore, fairy rings are where the fairies come to dance, and the leafy pendant beads on this cushion almost seem to revolve to the rhythm of the dance. The green fabrics and beads pick up the colours of a woodland glade, while the yellow beads suggest flickering sunlight.

Use beads in several different shapes and sizes for variety and texture. Here the pendant leaf beads and mother-of pearl doughnut beads work especially well.

the magic ingredients...

24 light green pendant leaf-shaped beads

5 x 2cm (¾in) green-dyed flat mother-of-pearl doughnut beads, or similar

7 x 6mm (¼in) smoky green pearl beads

16 x 6mm (¼in) lime green transparent plastic cube beads

30 x 6mm (¼in) green frosted glass beads

5g size 11 acid yellow rocailles

5g size 9 light green rocailles

40cm (½yd) of 90cm (36in) wide jade green silk dupion

15cm (6in) of 90cm (36in) wide light green silk taffeta

green sewing thread

jade green metallic machine embroidery thread

size 10 crewel embroidery needle

water-erasable fabric marker pen

30cm (12in) square cushion pad

1 Cut a 33 x 25cm (13¼ x 10in) rectangle of jade green silk dupion. Using the template on page 124 and the water-erasable pen, draw the dots of two large rings and two medium rings on the silk rectangle. Sew a leaf bead at each dot of the large circles with a double length of metallic thread using a size 10 embroidery needle, making sure that the leaves are pointing outwards.

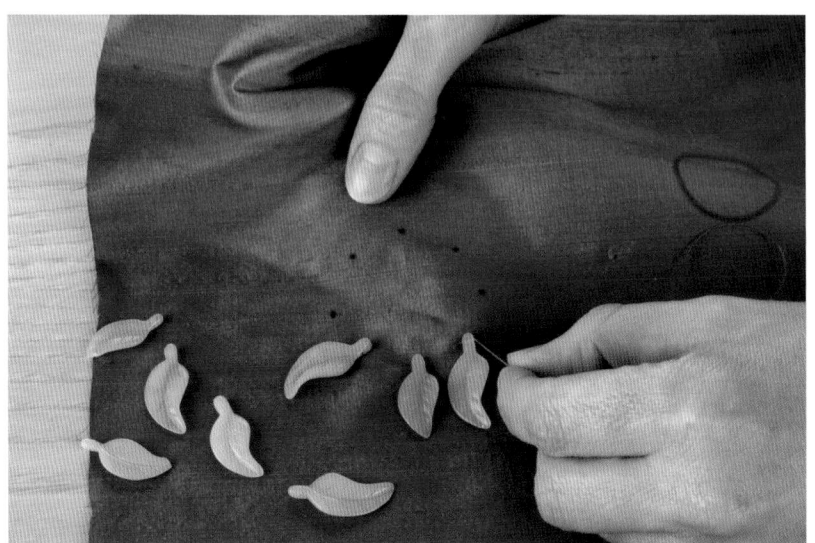

2 Bring the needle to the right side 3mm (⅛in) from the base of one leaf. Thread on a size 11 acid yellow rocaille, a lime green transparent plastic cube bead and another yellow rocaille. Lay the beads between the leaves and insert the needle back through the fabric after the last bead. Repeat to sew the rocaille beads and a cube bead between all the leaves.

words of wisdom...

When using ordinary sewing thread to attach beads, run it over some beeswax before you begin. This strengthens the thread and helps it slip more easily through both the fabric and beads.

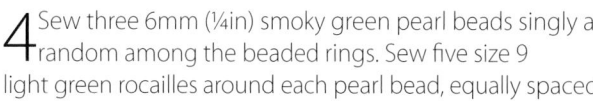

3 Still using metallic green thread, sew acid yellow rocaille beads along the circumference of the small circles about 2mm (1/6in) apart, as shown here.

4 Sew three 6mm (1/4in) smoky green pearl beads singly at random among the beaded rings. Sew five size 9 light green rocailles around each pearl bead, equally spaced.

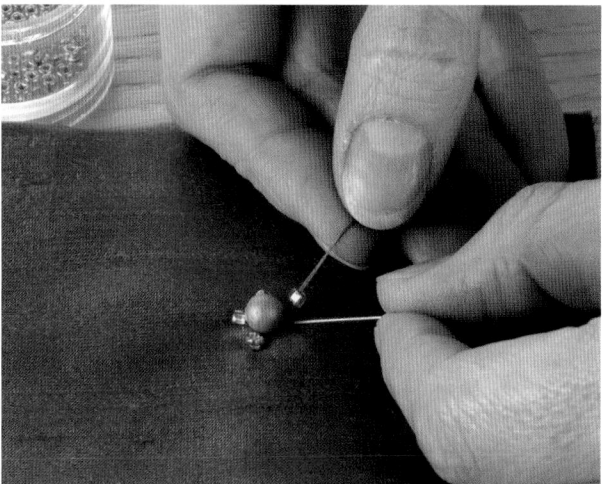

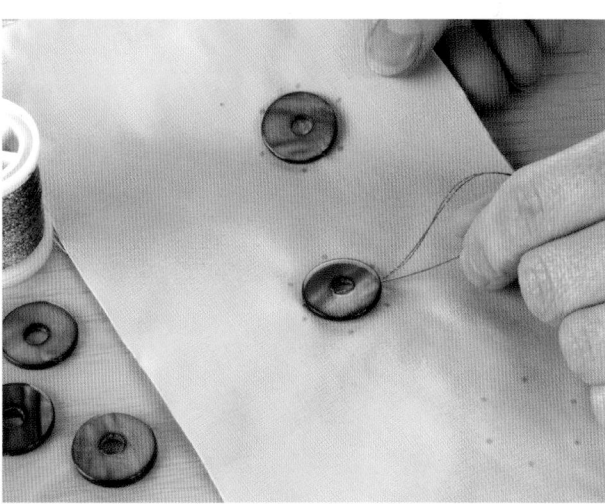

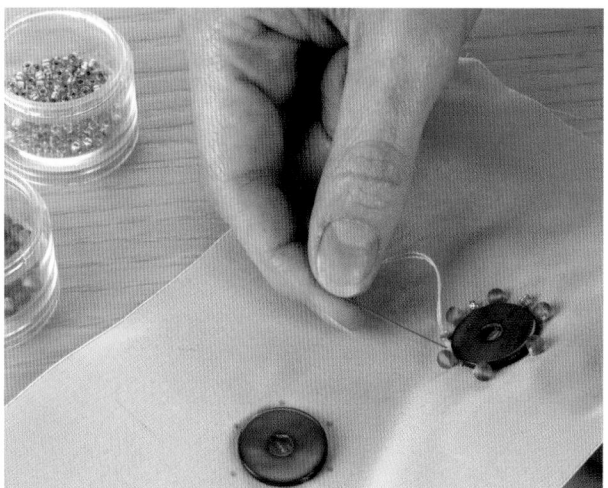

5 Cut a 33 x 11cm (13¼ x 4½in) rectangle of light green silk taffeta. Use the template to mark the dots of five small rings at random at least 2.5cm (1in) inside the raw edges on the silk rectangle with a water-erasable pen. Sew a mother-of-pearl doughnut bead in the centre of each ring of dots with a double length of jade green metallic machine embroidery thread.

6 Sew a 6mm (1/4in) green frosted glass bead at each dot around one of the mother-of-pearl beads. Sew a light green rocaille bead between each green glass bead. Repeat on all the other rings. With right sides facing, stitch the beaded rectangles together along one long edge, taking a 1.5cm (5/8in) seam allowance. This is the cushion front. Press the seam open.

7 Cut a 33cm (13¼in) square of jade green silk dupion for the cushion back. With right sides facing, stitch the front and back together along the outer edges, taking a 1.5cm (5/8in) seam allowance and leaving a 25cm (10in) gap in the lower edge. Clip the seam allowance across the corners, as shown. Turn right side out through the gap.

8 Sew acid yellow rocailles along the seam on the front of the cushion about 2mm (¹⁄₁₆in) apart, finishing 1.5cm (⁵⁄₈in) from the raw edge of the opening.

9 Bring the needle out at one corner. Thread on a 6mm (¹⁄₄in) smoky green pearl bead, 19 light green rocailles, a leaf bead and 4 light green rocailles.

10 Insert the needle back through the first 15 rocailles and the pearl and fasten the thread to the corner.

11 Insert the needle through the pearl bead. Thread on 13 light green rocailles, a leaf bead and 4 more rocailles. Insert the needle back through the first 9 rocailles and the pearl and fasten the thread to the corner.

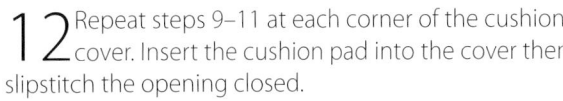

12 Repeat steps 9–11 at each corner of the cushion cover. Insert the cushion pad into the cover then slipstitch the opening closed.

words of wisdom...

If your cushion is likely to receive heavy wear – i.e. if there are children in the house – apply fusible interfacing to the back of the cushion front once the beading is completed. This secures the thread on the back of the fabric to ensure that if one bead comes loose others won't follow.

The beads on the corners of the cushion provide additional movement and help to unify the two fabric sections.

christmas snowflakes

These sparkling Christmas decorations are quick to make using ready-made wire forms. The stylized snowflakes are decorated with light-catching crystals and diamante rondelle spacers. A faceted crystal heart hangs from each one to swing and catch the glowing light of the fireside. Experiment with different coloured beads, perhaps using a combination of colours on a single snowflake.

These gleaming decorations are so simple to make that you could get the whole family involved in a crafting session. Kids will love the satisfaction of having made their own sparkling snowflakes to hang from the tree.

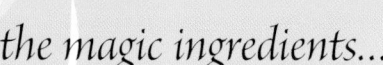

the magic ingredients...

12 pink diamante rondelle spacers

2 x 5mm (¼in) pink flat-backed jewel stones

24 x 8mm (5/16in) bicone crystals

2cm (¾in) heart-shaped crystal

silver pendant holder with a ring attached

10cm (4in) diameter snowflake wire form

90cm (1yd) silver knitting wire (optional)

30cm (12in) of 3mm (1/8in) wide pink ribbon

snipe-nose (flat-nose) pliers

round-nose pliers

tweezers

instant-bonding glue

words of wisdom...

Don't squeeze snipe-nose pliers too tightly around the pendant holder and heart-shaped crystal, as the surface of the delicate crystal may chip or scratch.

1 Glue a 5mm (¼in) flat-back pink jewel to the centre of the wire form with instant-bonding glue. A pair of tweezers is invaluable here. Turn the wire form over and stick another stone on the centre, exactly behind the first stone.

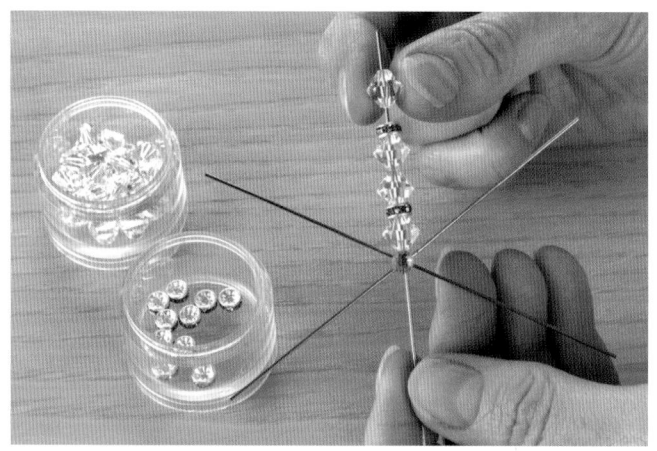
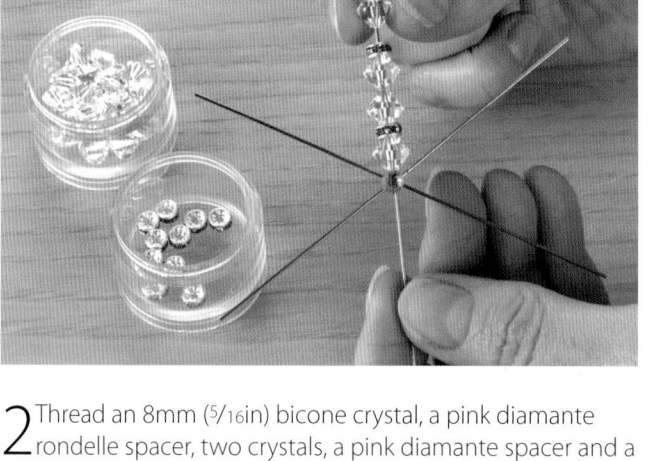

2 Thread an 8mm (5/16in) bicone crystal, a pink diamante rondelle spacer, two crystals, a pink diamante spacer and a crystal onto an arm of the wire form, as shown.

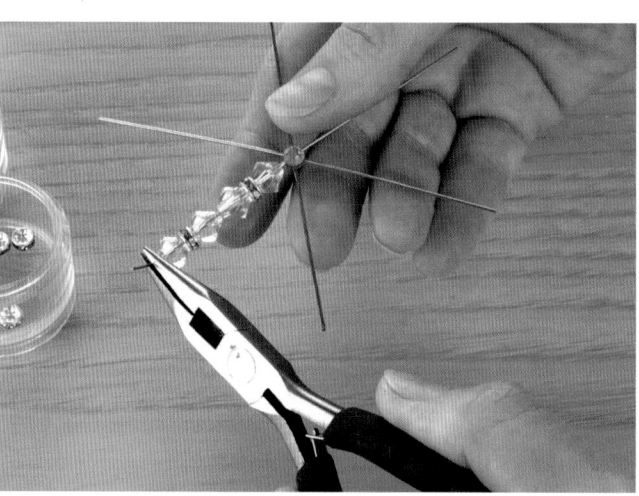

3 Bend the wire above the last crystal forward at a 45-degree angle using your snipe-nose pliers.

4 Grasp the wire just above the bend with the round-nose pliers and twist the wire around it to make a loop.

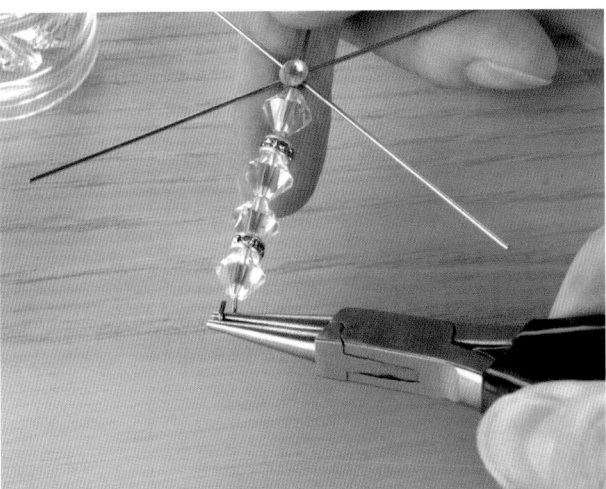

5 Repeat steps 2–4 to embellish each arm of the wire form using the same arrangement of beads.

6 Slip a heart-shaped crystal onto the prongs of the pendant holder. Squeeze the pendant holder closed with the snipe-nose pliers.

7 Using round-nose pliers, open the loop at the bottom of the decoration. Slip the ring of the pendant holder onto the loop then close it again.

8 Thread ribbon through the loop at the top of the decoration so you can hang it up. For added embellishment, bind a length of silver knitting wire tightly around one of the arms between the first crystal and rondelle spacer. Wrap it once around the next arm then around the next, and so on. To secure the end, wrap it tightly around the first arm and snip off the excess. Repeat to wrap further 'rings' of wire just above each crystal.

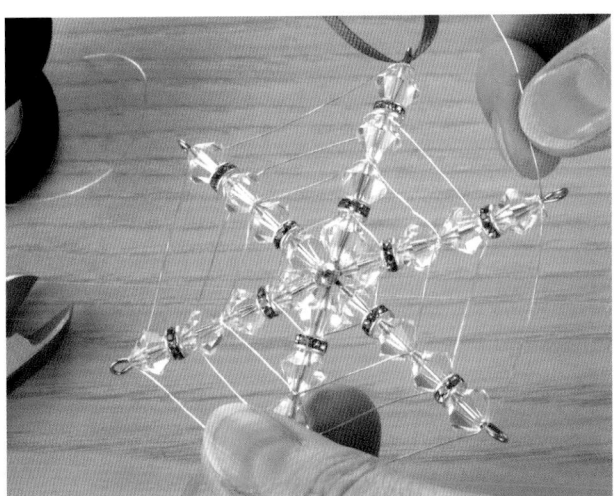

tooth-fairy box

The story of the tooth fairy is one of the loveliest family traditions. The idea is that in return for a baby tooth, which the fairy can put to good use, she leaves behind a coin or small gift. Get the child to pop the tooth inside for the fairy to claim during the night. Alternatively, use the box to store trinkets or use it as a stunning gift box for a small brooch, ring or beaded earrings.

No tooth fairy could resist the temptation to peep inside this lovely box made from card, wadding, fabric and beads. For the ultimate in luxury, use silk fabrics in place of the cotton ones.

the magic ingredients...

rocaille beads:
4 size 7 gold
9 size 9 gold
5g size 11 purple glass
5g size 11 aquamarine

4 x 1.5cm (⁵/₈in) purple spear-shaped drop beads for the wings

5mm (¼in) purple heart-shaped bead

20cm (8in) square of aquamarine-spotted white cotton fabric

20cm (8in) square of plain aquamarine cotton fabric

20cm (8in) square of 50g (2oz) wadding

air-erasable fabric marker pen

white sewing thread

size 10 embroidery needle

thin card

fabric glue

glue spreader

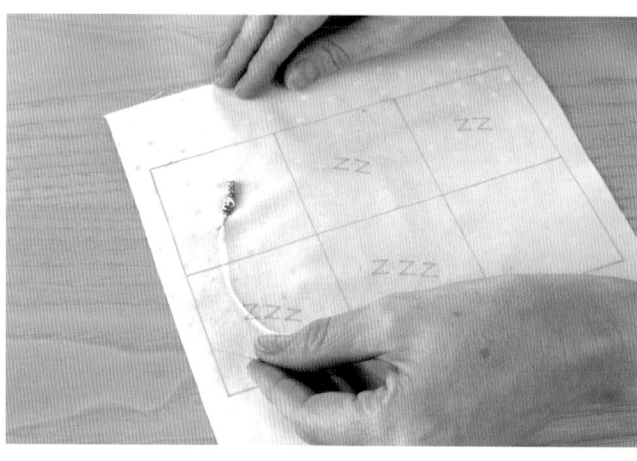

1 Draw six 6cm (2³/₈in) squares on the spotted white cotton fabric with an air-erasable fabric marker pen. Refer to the template on page 124 to draw the dragonfly body on 1 square, ZZ on 2 squares and ZZZ on another 2 squares.

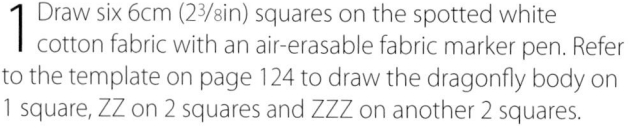

2 Starting at the wide end of the dragonfly body, use a double length of sewing thread to sew four size 7 gold rocaille beads then nine size 9 gold rocaille beads along the body of the dragonfly with backstitch. Sew two purple 1.5cm (⁵/₈in) spear-shaped drop beads on each side of the body at the thick end as wings. Fasten the thread ends securely on the wrong side.

3 Bring the needle to the right side on the end of a ZZ. Thread on enough size 11 purple rocaille beads to fit the top line of the first Z. Make a tiny stitch at the end of the line and insert the needle back through the last bead. Thread on enough purple rocaille beads to fit along the diagonal line. Make a tiny stitch at the end and insert the needle back through the last bead as before. Continue to the end of the first Z then complete all the Zs in the same way. Cut out the squares.

4 Cut six 4cm (1⅝in) squares of thin card and five 4cm (1⅝in) squares of wadding. Glue each wadding square to a card square with fabric glue, using a glue spreader to spread the glue evenly.

5 Place the remaining card square centrally on the wrong side of the un-beaded fabric square. Stick the corners and then the edges of the fabric to the back of the card with fabric glue and leave to dry. Place the padded card squares centrally, wadding side down on the wrong side of the beaded squares of fabric. Glue the fabric to the padded card in the same way as before. Leave these to dry thoroughly before proceeding to step 6.

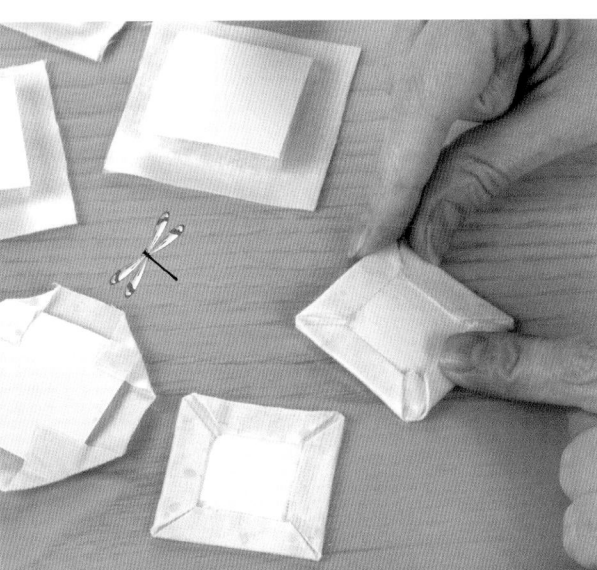

6 Cut six 5.7cm (2¼in) squares of aquamarine cotton fabric for the box lining. Cut six 3.7cm (1½in) squares of thin card and wadding. Glue wadding to each card square and cover with fabric as before. Stick the lining to the underside of the box squares.

7 Hold one ZZ square and one ZZZ square together at right angles with side edges meeting. Slipstitch the edges securely together, catching in a size 11 aquamarine rocaille bead with each stitch. Repeat to join the other ZZ and ZZZ squares to form the box sides.

8 Slipstitch the plain box square to the lower edge of the box to form the base, as shown. Do not bead the edges of the box base because beads here may prevent the box from standing straight and they will hardly show here.

9 Bring the needle out at the centre upper edge of the box front. Thread on five size 11 purple glass rocaille beads, a 5mm (¼in) purple heart-shaped bead and a purple rocaille bead. Insert the needle back through all the beads except the last. Knot securely.

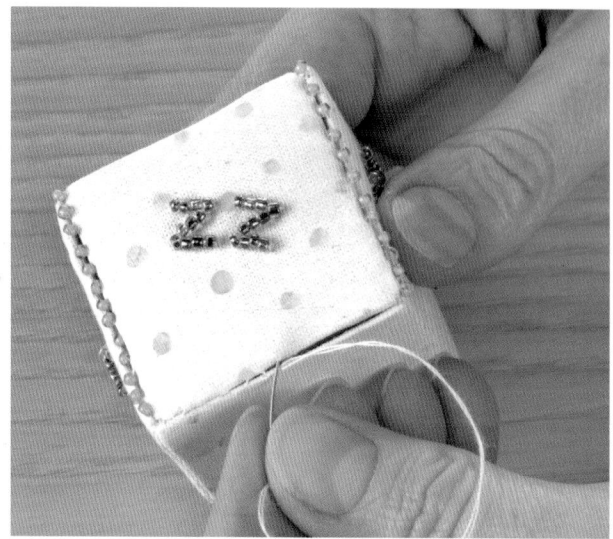

10 To create the picot beaded edge on the lid, bring the needle out close one corner. Thread on three aquamarine rocaille beads. Insert the needle into the edge of the lid 2mm (1/16in) from where it emerged and bring it out 4mm (1/8in) further on; repeat around the edge of the lid. Make small knots at intervals for security.

11 Slipstitch the back edge of the lid to the box back. Bring the needle out at the front edge of the lid 1.5cm (5/8in) from one corner. Thread on enough gold rocaille beads to loop around the hanging beads. Fasten the thread 1.5cm (5/8in) from the opposite corner. Thread the needle back through the beads to secure the loop.

words of wisdom...
The dragonfly on the lid is surprisingly easy to make using spear-shaped drop beads for the wings. It would look great anywhere – add it to an embroidery or use it on a small thank-you card.

lavender bag

To complement the tooth-fairy box, make this lovely
lavender bag to help encourage a good night's sleep.
Cut two 14.5cm (5¾in) squares of fine linen. At the
centre of one piece stitch three bunched stems in
backstitch, catching a mid green Delica bead in each
stitch. Thread on enough beads to pass over the stems
to form a tie with a single stitch. For the flower heads
use size 11 cylindrical purple beads. Now stitch the
two linen squares together, taking a 5mm (¼in) seam
allowance, leaving an opening to turn in the top edge.
Clip the seam allowances at the corners then turn
the sachet out and press it. Stitch an inner square to
create a 2cm (¾in) border, leaving an opening at the
top. Now simply fill with dried lavender and stitch the
openings closed. As a final touch, stitch single green
Delica beads around the inner square.

blackberry candleholder

Entwined with luscious beaded blackberries, this glass candleholder brings the subtle beauty of the hedgerow into the home throughout the year. Light the candle in moments of quiet contemplation and enjoy the romance of the jewel-like berries in the flickering light. Ideally use a glass candleholder with tapering sides so that the ends of the blackberry stalks can curl around and under the base.

Re-create the sheen of ripe, juicy blackberries by using black and iridescent rocaille beads for the luscious fruits.

the magic ingredients...

4 brick-red 1.5cm (5/8in) long oval beads

8g of size 9 black rocaille beads

4g of size 9 iridescent black rocaille beads

12 x 1.2cm (½in) raspberry-red bugle beads

1m (1¼yds) of 0.9mm leaf-green enamelled wire

3m (3½yds) of 0.315mm leaf-green enamelled wire

green paper

glass candleholder

purple Nymo thread

size 10 beading needle

thick needle

instant-bonding glue

all-purpose household glue

wire snips

cocktail stick

masking tape

artist's paintbrush (see step 12)

words of wisdom...

You don't have to use a clear glass candleholder for this project. You could try green or red glass, for example.

1 Thread a 90cm (36in) double length of purple Nymo thread onto a size 10 beading needle and knot the ends together. Insert the needle through a brick-red 1.5cm (5/8in) long oval bead and slip the needle between the threads. Pull the needle to suspend the bead. Dab the knot sparingly with instant-bonding glue and adjust the knot to hide it in the bead.

2 Mix size 9 black and iridescent black rocaille beads together. Thread on enough rocailles to fit around one side of the oval bead and insert the needle back through the hole in the oval bead.

3 Insert the needle through the first two beads. Thread on 4 less beads than the first row. Insert the needle through the last two beads of the first row. Insert the needle back through the oval bead.

4 Repeat steps 2–3 to cover the oval bead. To finish, weave the thread through a few rows of beads and cut off the excess thread. Make another three beaded blackberries in the same way.

5 Use wire snips to snip one 30cm (12in), one 25cm (10in) and one 20cm (8in) length of 0.9mm leaf-green enamelled wire. Dab instant-bonding glue on one end of each length of wire and insert it into a bead for the stalk.

6 Use the template on page 124 to cut four sets of sepals from green paper. Pierce a hole in the centre of the sepals with a thick needle. Insert a stalk through the hole in each set of sepals. Apply all-purpose household glue to the sepals with a cocktail stick and press against the base of the blackberry. Leave the glue to dry.

7 Wrap the stalks around the candleholder, tape the wires together with masking tape and press them under the base. Snip the ends of the wires level. Remove the blackberries, keeping the wire in shape.

words of wisdom...
Save time and cut the sepals out of green paper using any small star punch.

8 Snip four 75cm (30in) lengths of 0.315mm leaf-green enamelled wire. Hold the lengths together at one end and bind them around the stalks, starting at the stalk ends. Dab with instant-bonding glue to hold all the ends together. Discard the masking tape as you reach it.

9 Stop binding the four stalks at the point where they splay apart. Take one of the 0.315mm wires you have been using to wind the stem and bind it around one of the stalks to about 4cm (1½in) from the blackberry, as shown below.

10 Thread on a bugle bead. Push it along the binding wire to the stalk. Fold the wire over the bugle bead.

11 Twist the wire on itself twice under the bugle bead. Repeat to add two more bugle beads.

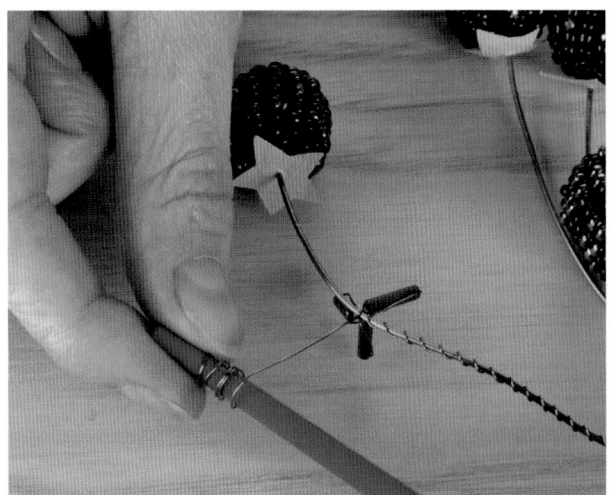

12 Snip the extending end of the wire 10cm (4in) from the stalk. To make a tendril, bind the end of the wire around the handle of an artist's paintbrush. Remove the paintbrush. Gently pull open the tendril. Repeat steps 9–12 to finish all the blackberry stalks. Wrap the blackberry sprig around the candleholder again.

blackcurrant napkin ring

If you wish to use the blackberry candleholder
as a table centrepiece, coordinate with a set of
napkin rings. First make the ring by holding
four 50cm (20in) lengths of 0.9mm green
enamelled wire together and coiling them around
a napkin. Remove the napkin. Starting 4cm
(1½in) from one end, bind a 190cm (75in) length
of 0.315mm green enamelled wire around the
thick wires. Every so often thread on 20 purple
rocaille beads for a leaf. Bend the beaded wire
into a ring and twist both wires together twice.
Squeeze the beaded ring to make a leaf shape.
Continue binding the thick wires and adding
leaves until 4cm (1½in) from the ends. Splay open
the thick wires and glue each wire inside an 8mm
(5/16in) black bead with instant-bonding glue.
Unravel some string. Glue the end into each
black bead. Leave to dry then cut the string
3mm (1/8in) above the beads.

magical greetings

A simple motif can be interpreted in beads on your greetings cards – it's a wonderful way of adding a personal, artistic touch. The beads are attached with backstitch and an insert within each card hides the back of the picture – it couldn't be easier. These cards would be lovely for Valentine's Day, or for a little girl's birthday. Choose an attractive printed paper for the greetings cards that complements your design, or embellish plain paper yourself.

Personalize your card by using the recipient's favourite colour and, if desired, add a bead in their birthstone colour, as on the pink and grey card here.

the magic ingredients...

2g size 11 navy blue
cylinder beads

1 x 6mm (¼in) turquoise
heart-shaped bead

assorted turquoise beads
with large holes

16cm (6¼in) square of pale
pink fabric

grey/pink patterned paper

pale pink card

mottled grey paper

130cm (51in) fine pink cord

small embroidery hoop

beading needle and size 10
embroidery needle

navy blue sewing thread

masking and double-sided tape

iron and cotton towel

spray adhesive and glue stick

craft knife and cutting mat

metal ruler

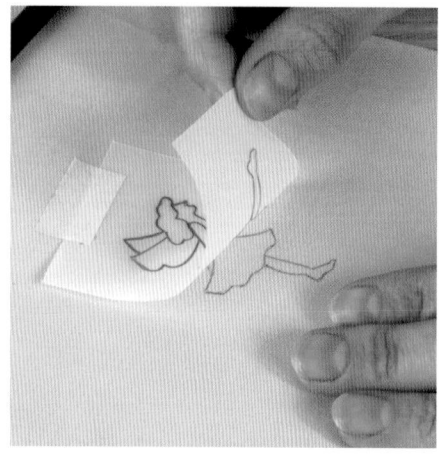

1 Trace the fairy silhouette template on page 125 onto tracing paper with a sharp pencil. Turn the tracing over and redraw it on the wrong side. Tape the tracing right side up on the centre of your pale pink fabric and redraw the design to transfer it.

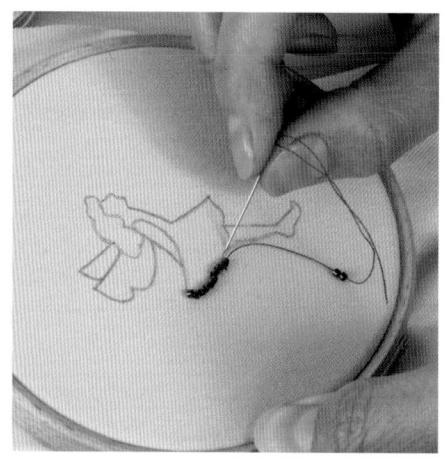

2 Stretch the fabric in the hoop. Using a beading needle and navy thread, secure the thread on the wrong side of the fabric and bring the needle to the right side on the hem of the dress. Sew size 11 navy cylinder beads along the outlines in backstitch, threading on two beads at a time.

3 Sew the heart-shaped bead to the fairy behind her hands. Remove the fabric from the hoop and press the fabric around fairy using a towel to cushion the beading. Cut the fabric into a 10 x 8cm (4 x 3¼in) rectangle of the fabric with the fairy at the centre.

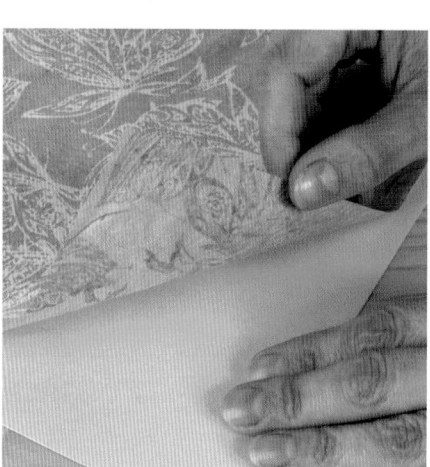

4 Apply grey/pink printed paper to pale pink card with spray adhesive. Resting on a cutting mat, cut a 22 x 20cm (8½ x 8in) rectangle of the covered card with a craft knife. Score and fold the card in half to make a card 11 x 20cm (4¼ x 8in) using the back of the craft knife blade. Open the card out flat.

words of wisdom...

Before you peel off the backing of the double-sided tape, lightly mark in pencil where the corners of the fabric should sit on the inside of the card to ensure the fairy is central in the aperture.

5 For the aperture, draw a 7 x 5cm (2¾ x 2in) rectangle centrally on the wrong side of the card front 3cm (1¼in) down from the upper edge. Cut out the rectangle, as shown.

6 Apply double-sided tape around the aperture on the wrong side. Peel off the backing tapes and carefully position and stick the fabric rectangle over the aperture.

7 Cut a 21 x 19cm (8¼ x 7½in) rectangle of mottled grey paper for the insert. Fold the paper in half so it is 10.5 x 19cm (4⅛ x 7½in). Run a line of paper glue along the fold and stick the insert inside the card, matching the folds.

 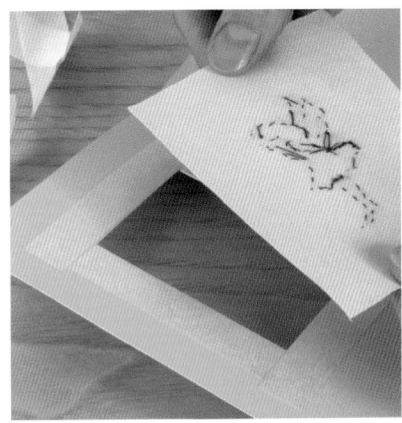 

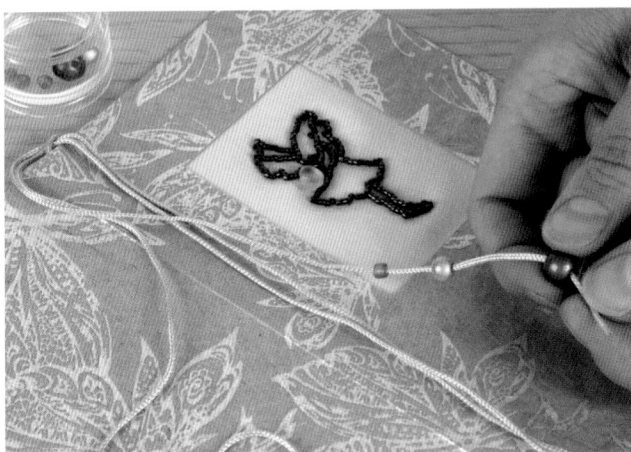

8 Bend a length of pink cord in half and lay it over the card with the bend at the top. Fold the ends up inside the cord and pull them to the outside through the loop at the top of the cord. Slip turquoise beads on each end. Knot the cord under the beads and cut off the excess. It is helpful if you dab the ends of the cord with clear glue – this makes them easier to thread through the beads and prevents the cord from fraying.

spell binding

This vibrant fairy carrying a magic wand is created in a similar way. The dress, wings and face are cut from bright and pale pink fabric, and applied to blue fabric with fusible webbing. The hair is two rows of 4mm (5/32in) silver sequins and the face, dress and wings are outlined in backstitch with size 11 pink rocaille beads. The arms and legs are single bead strands, with oval pink beads for feet; the arms are also single strands of beads. The wand is a stitch of metallic pink embroidery thread, catching a star sequin at the top. More sequins are sewn to the dress and around the wand. The card is made of glittery pink printed paper applied to deep pink card. It is 30 x 13cm (12 x 5in), scored and folded in half. The beaded fairy is stuck behind a 10 x 6.5cm (4 x 2½in) aperture.

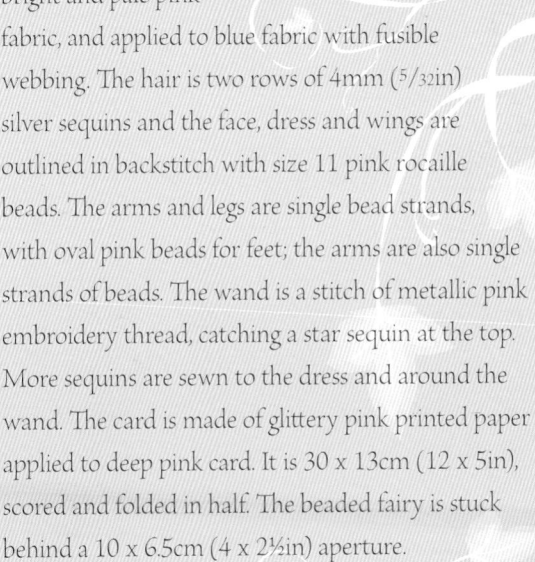

59

beautiful
beaded
butterflies

Make a trio of prettily beaded butterflies to hang

from a hook or twig, or to flutter at a window or

hover around a mirror. Each butterfly is embroidered

onto silk and has fine wire antennae. The instructions

given here are for making a pink and white butterfly;

change the colour scheme as you wish.

Make a whole family of
butterflies in different
colours – it will be
difficult to choose your
favourite.

2 x 6mm (¼in) pink
plastic beads

4 x 8mm (5/16in) pink
plastic beads

4g of 4mm (1/8in) pink
bugle beads

about 110 x 5mm (¼in)
transparent lilac cup sequins

4g of size 11 aquamarine
rocaille beads

2g of size 11 gold |
rocaille beads

2g of size 11 silver
rocaille beads

30cm (12in) square of white
silk dupion

30cm (12in) square of firm
iron-on interfacing

22cm (8½in) embroidery hoop

15 x 12cm (6 x 5in) rectangle of
fusible webbing

water-erasable fabric
marker pen

size 10 embroidery needle

matching sewing thread

15cm (6in) of 0.4mm silver wire

1.5cm (5/8in) curtain ring

suction cup hook (optional)

round-nose pliers

sharp scissors

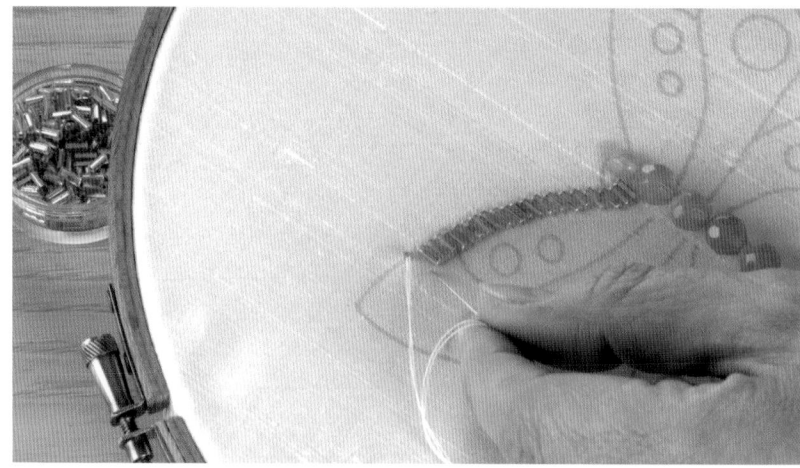

1 Trace the butterfly from page 125 onto silk dupion with a water-erasable fabric marking pen, omitting the dot, then fuse firm iron-on interfacing to the back of the silk with an iron. Fix the silk in an embroidery hoop. With a double length of thread, sew a 6mm (¼in) pink plastic bead, four 8mm (5/16in) pink plastic beads and another 6mm (¼in) pink plastic bead along the centre of the butterfly using backstitch. Sew bugle beads side by side along the upper edges of the wings, as shown.

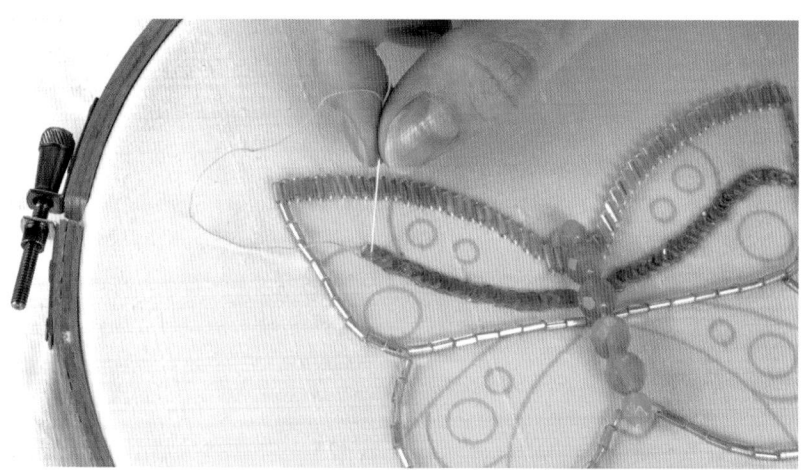

2 Sew bugle beads along the remaining outlines of the wings with backstitch, referring to the picture here to position them correctly. Sew overlapping sequins to the upper wings, as explained on page 19, matching the top of the sequins to the long drawn line.

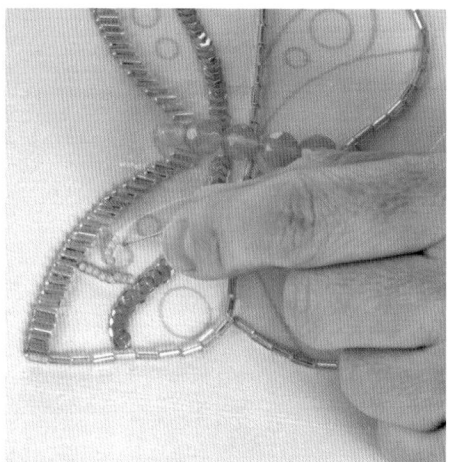

3 Sew aquamarine rocaille beads along the remaining drawn lines and outline the circles on the upper wings, again using backstitch. Fill in the circles with aquamarine beads sewn on singly. Now outline the circles on the lower wings with gold rocaille beads using backstitch then fill them with gold beads sewn on singly. Sew silver rocaille beads at random in the outer sections of the wings.

4 Using sharp scissors, cut out the butterfly carefully, adding a 1cm (³/₈in) allowance all round. Turn the allowance to the underside, snipping the curves and corners so that the fabric lays flat. Now sew the seam allowance in place on the back, hiding the stitches under the beading as far as possible.

5 Bend the 0.4mm silver wire in half, then bend the ends of the wire outwards for the antennae. Thread an aquamarine rocaille bead onto one end of the wire and tightly coil the end of the wire to secure the bead in place using round-nose pliers. Repeat on the other end of the wire. Lay the antennae along the centre of the butterfly on the wrong side as shown, and stitch in place.

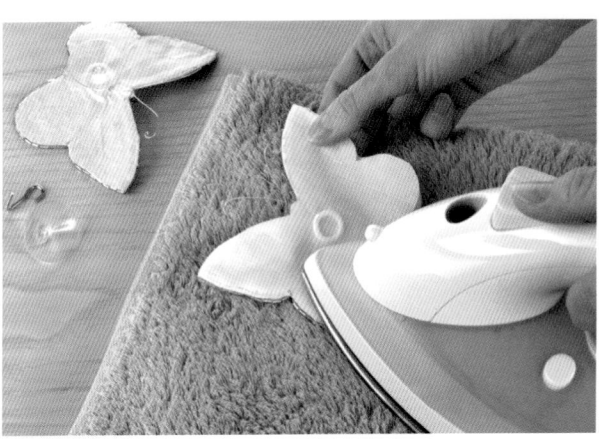

6 Draw a butterfly on the paper backing of a piece of fusible webbing. Cut out the butterfly, leaving a margin all round. Fuse the butterfly to the remaining silk dupion with an iron. Cut out the butterfly, just inside the drawn line then peel off the backing paper. Sew the top of a curtain ring to the silk backing at the dot.

7 Place the beaded butterfly face down on a folded towel to protect the beads. Position the silk backing, adhesive side down on top. Iron the butterflies to fuse them together. If you wish to stick the butterfly to glass or a mirror, remove the hook from the suction cup. Push the top of the suction cup through the curtain ring. Moisten the suction cup to stick it to glass.

words of wisdom...

Take your inspiration from nature, and look for pictures or photographs of butterflies that you like. Trace the picture, simplifying the design as you do so, then stitch the butterfly using beads and sequins in the appropriate colours. You can also work on coloured fabric to speed things along and to add impact.

toadstool charms

Wherever there is magic you'll find red spotted toadstools – in stories and paintings, on statues, carvings and more. You'll need a toadstool for your enchanted theme too, and this pretty beaded version is just perfect. Made from red and opal crystal beads, the shimmering toadstool is hung from a key ring that you could use for your keys or hang on a handbag, mobile phone or any other item as a fairy decoration.

The red and white toadstool is the Fly Agaric (Amanita muscaria), a poisonous toadstool common in Britain and mainland Europe but, as you can see, any colour combinations are possible.

the magic ingredients...

22 x light Siam (red) 4mm (¹/₈in) round faceted crystals

4 x white opal 4mm (¹/₈in) round faceted crystals

8 x Pacific (blue) opal 4mm (¹/₈in) round faceted crystals

bead to use as a stop bead

8mm (⁵/₁₆in) silver jump ring

key ring

red quilting thread

size 10 beading needle

snipe-nose (flat-nose) pliers

1 Cut a 120cm (48in) length of quilting thread and fit a stop bead at one end (shown in blue), leaving a 20cm (8in) trailing end (see page 22). For the first row, thread on four light Siam crystals. Thread on another light Siam crystal, which will be on the second row (bead 5). Hold bead 5 under bead 4. Insert the thread through bead 4, as shown.

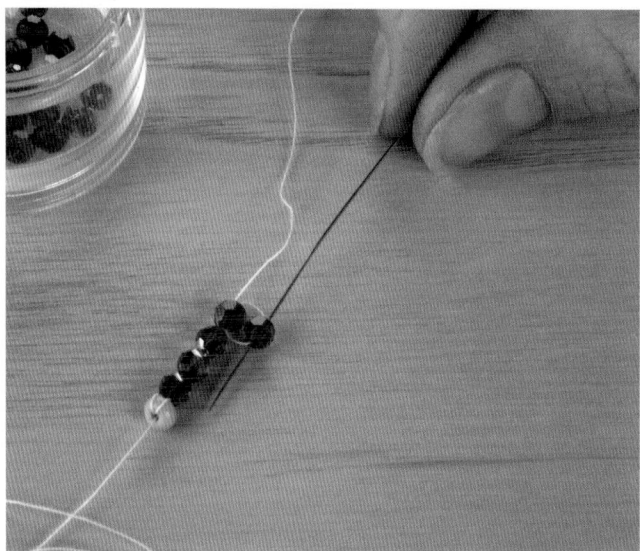

2 Now pass the thread through bead 5 again. You are beginning a weaving stitch known as square stitch. Refer to pages 22–23 for further instructions if you need them and see below for a chart for this design.

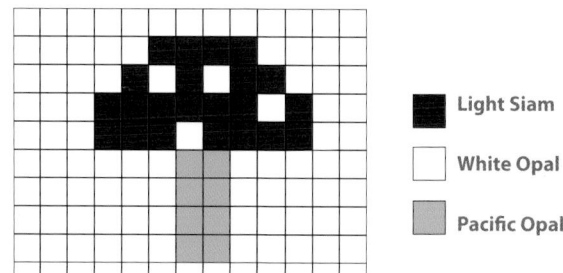

■ **Light Siam**

□ **White Opal**

▨ **Pacific Opal**

3 Thread on a white opal bead to represent one of the spots of the toadstool and insert the needle through the second from last crystal on the first row (bead 3), as shown below.

4 Insert the needle through the bead just added (bead 6). Repeat the process to add a light Siam crystal and a white opal bead (beads 7 and 8). Insert the needle through all the beads on the first row.

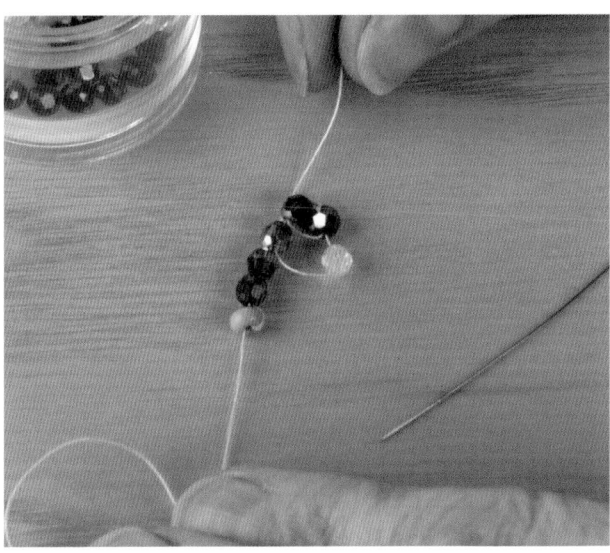

5 Insert the needle through the beads on the second row. Thread on one light Siam crystal (bead 9).

6 Turn the thread and thread on another light Siam crystal (bead 10) Hold bead 10 under bead 9. Insert the needle through bead 9 in the same way as before.

words of wisdom...

Read through all the instructions before you begin because the beads aren't necessarily added in the order that you might expect.

7 Insert the needle through bead 10 again. Add 4 light Siam crystals, inserting the needle through the bead above after each one as before. Thread on a white opal bead. Turn the thread and thread on one light Siam crystal, which will be the last bead of the second row. Insert the needle through the white opal bead.

8 Thread the needle through the second and third row. To make the fourth row, add 3 light Siam crystals, a white opal bead and 2 light Siam crystals in the same way as before. Thread on a light Siam bead, which will be the first bead of the fourth row. Turn the thread and thread on a light Siam crystal – the first bead of the third row.

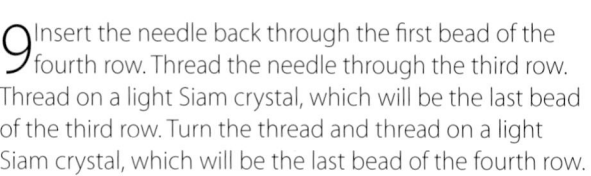

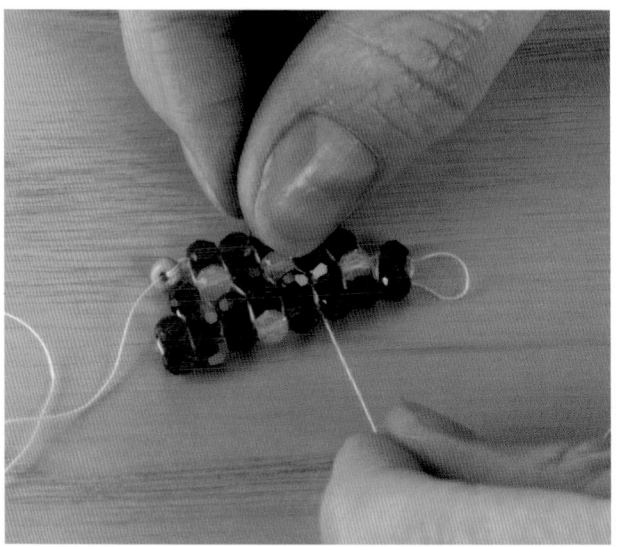

9 Insert the needle back through the first bead of the fourth row. Thread the needle through the third row. Thread on a light Siam crystal, which will be the last bead of the third row. Turn the thread and thread on a light Siam crystal, which will be the last bead of the fourth row.

10 Insert the needle through the last bead on the third row. Thread the needle through the fourth and third row then thread the needle through the last 3 beads of the fourth row, as shown.

11 To make the stalk, thread on a Pacific opal bead. Insert the needle through the fifth bead of the fourth row then through the Pacific opal. Thread on another Pacific opal. Insert the needle through the fourth bead on the fourth row. Insert the needle through the last bead again then through the fourth and fifth bead of the fourth and fifth row. Make another 3 rows.

12 Remove the stop bead from the start of the beading. Weave the thread ends through the beads for a few rows and cut off the excess thread. Hold a jump ring with a pair of snipe-nose (flat-nose) pliers, twist it open and fix it between the middle beads on the first row. Slip a key ring onto the jump ring, as shown, then close the ring to finish.

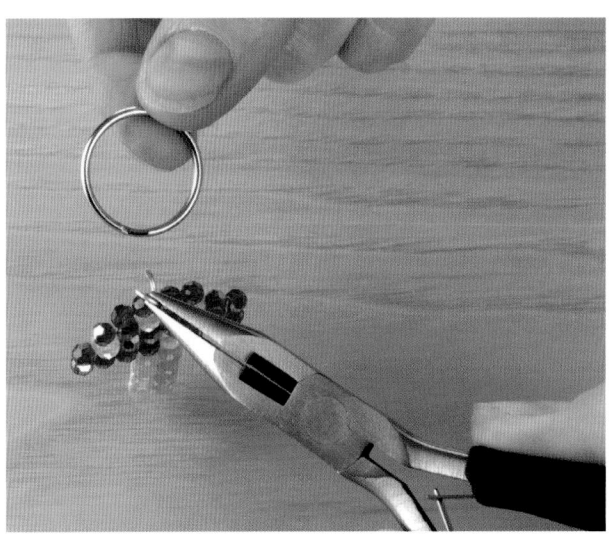

words of wisdom...

A toadstool would make a lovely necklace medallion. Just omit the key ring and fit the jump ring to a plain gold or silver necklace chain or even a leather thong.

Make a green toadstool using blue zircon crystal beads with jet crystal spots and a silver crystal bead stalk. Place the spots wherever you like.

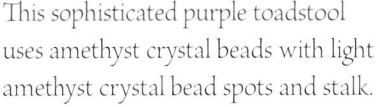

This sophisticated purple toadstool uses amethyst crystal beads with light amethyst crystal bead spots and stalk.

fairy princess

This beautiful fairy is fun to make and can be created from oddments and leftovers from other projects. She can sit up or be suspended on a thread, and her arms are beads threaded onto wire so that they can be bent into different positions. The flamboyant hair is created with boucle yarn to give the impression of tumbling curls but you can use other yarns for different looks (see page 75).

If you create a fairy princess to give as a gift, choose a colour of yarn to resemble the hair colour of the recipient.

the magic ingredients...

rocaille beads:
2 size 11 dark blue matt
2g size 9 turquoise glass

sequins:
3 x 1.2cm (½in) dark pink flowers
2 x 1.2cm (½in) pale pink flowers
8mm (⁵/₁₆in) orange stars
2 x 6mm (¼in) flowers
6 x 8mm (⁵/₁₆in) assorted flowers

cylinder beads:
2g size 9 pale pink
18 size 11 white frosted

metallic beads:
2 x 8mm (¼in) turquoise

assorted pink, turquoise and
crystal 4–6mm (about ¼in) beads
and crystals

assorted rock crystal chips

at least 20cm (8in) square of flesh
pink cotton fabric

at least 20cm (8in) square each of
cream and pink organza

at least 20 x 10cm (8 x 4in)
rectangle of blue organza

30cm (12in) of 0.4mm silver
wire and wire snips

size 10 beading needle

pink sewing thread

brown boucle wool

9cm (3½in) square of fusible
webbing

water- or air-erasable fabric
marker pen

pencil

pink fabric paint and fine
artist's paintbrush

toy filling

pinking shears

fabric glue

1 Use the template on page 125 to draw two fairies on flesh pink cotton fabric with the fabric pen; mark the broken lines on the wrong side of one fairy. With a sharp pencil, lightly draw the face on the right side of the other fairy. Paint the mouth with a fine artist's paintbrush using pink fabric paint. Set aside to dry then iron the fabric following the paint manufacturer's instructions. With right sides facing, stitch the fairies together along the broken lines, leaving the lower edge open in the centre. Clip the curves of the seam allowances and turn right sides out.

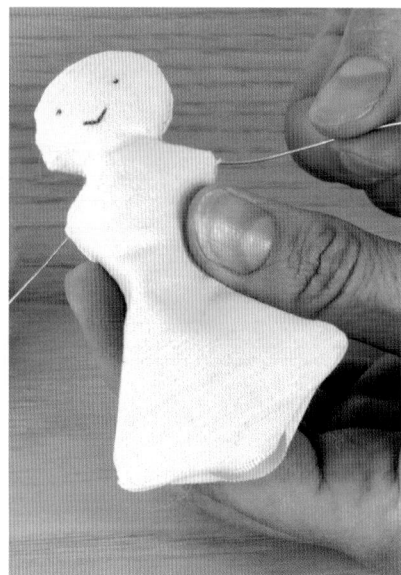

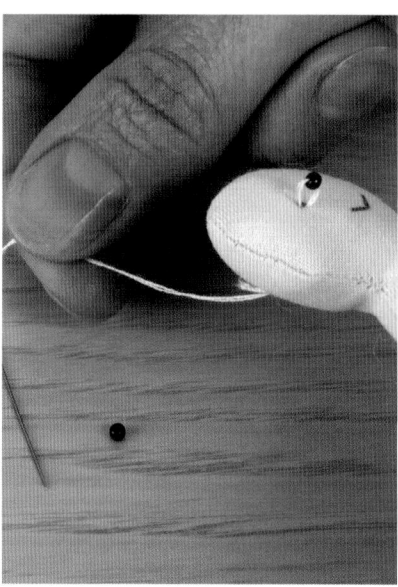

2 Stuff the head, neck and shoulders firmly with toy filling. For the arms, carefully insert the wire into the seam at one dot and out of the other. Continue stuffing the fairy firmly. Slipstitch the opening at the lower edge closed.

3 To make the eyes, knot a single length of sewing thread on a needle, insert the needle through the back of the head and bring it out through the dot for one eye. Thread on a size 11 dark blue matt rocaille bead. Insert the needle back through the eye and out through the back of the head, pull the thread so that the bead makes an indentation. Repeat with the other eye. Fasten the thread on the back of the head.

4 With pinking shears, cut an 8 x 5cm (3¼ x 2in) rectangle of pink organza for the bodice. Press the bodice in half along the length. Wrap the bodice tightly around the body with the upper folded edge level with the wire arms. Overlap the ends at the back and sew in place.

5 Thread a 1.2cm (½in) dark pink flower-shaped sequin onto the right arm wire. Thread on assorted beads, rock crystal chips and crystals for 4.5cm (1¾in). Thread on a 6mm (¼in) pink bead. Adjust the wire so that 3cm (1¼in) extends beyond the last bead. Bend the extending wire over the last bead then bind it tightly twice around the arm wire between the last two beads. Carefully snip off the excess wire close to the beads, ensuring no sharp ends are left.

6 Repeat step 5 on the other arm, there will be a longer length of wire extending – this is for the wand. Do not snip the wire yet. Bend the extending wire upwards. Thread on 18 size 11 white frosted cylinder beads, a 1.2cm (½in) dark pink flower-shaped sequin and an 8mm (5/16in) orange star-shaped sequin. Bend the wire downwards in front of the star and wrap it twice around the wand between two frosted beads. Snip off the excess wire close to the wand.

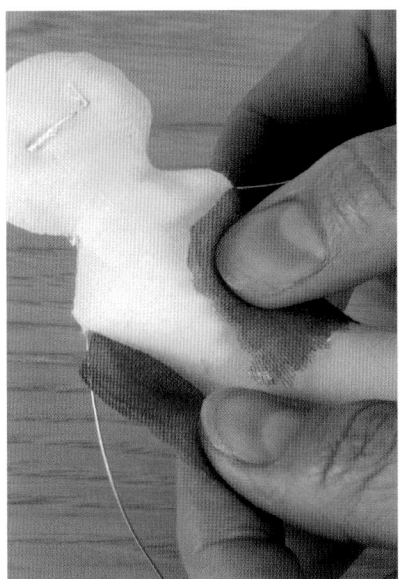

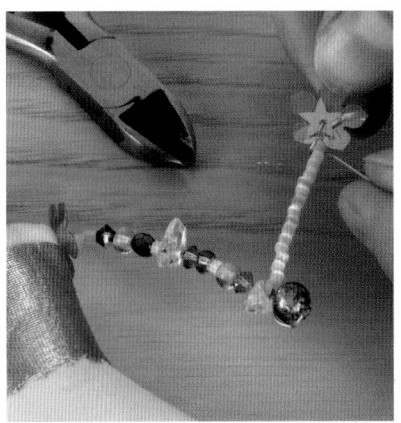

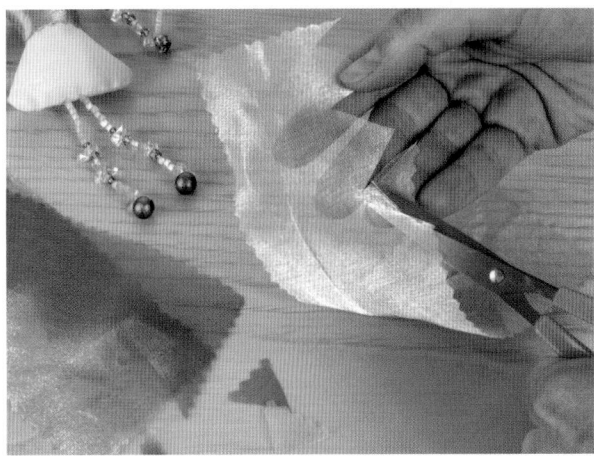

7 To make each leg, attach a double length of thread to the lower edge of the fairy, 5mm (¼in) from the centre. Thread on assorted beads, rock crystal chips and crystals for 5.5cm (2¼in). Thread on an 8mm (5/16in) turquoise metallic bead. Insert the needle back through all the beads except the last one and pull the thread so the beads lie close together and side by side.

8 Use pinking shears to cut a 20 x 5cm (8 x 2in) rectangle of blue organza, a 20 x 6.5cm (8 x 2½in) rectangle of cream organza and a 20 x 7cm (8 x 2¾in) rectangle of pink organza for the skirt. Cut a raggedy edge along the long, lower edges.

9 Pin the skirts together along the long, upper edges, placing the skirts one on top of the other increasing in size. Gather the upper edge. Pin the skirt around the waist, pulling up the gathers to fit and overlapping the ends at the back. Sew in place at the waist, catching in a size 9 turquoise glass rocaille bead with each stitch.

10 Cut about 11 lengths of brown boucle wool for the hair, each 14cm (5½in) long. Starting at the top of the head, sew the middle of each length of wool along the centre of the head with a backstitch. Use fabric glue sparingly to stick the hair around the face and to the back of the head until you have achieved the desired effect.

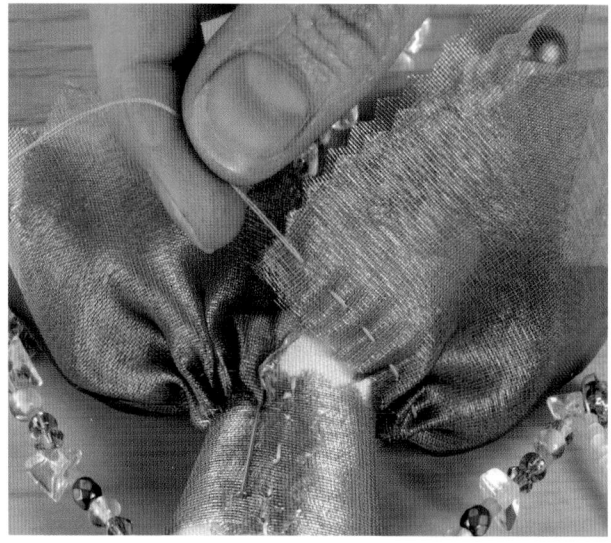

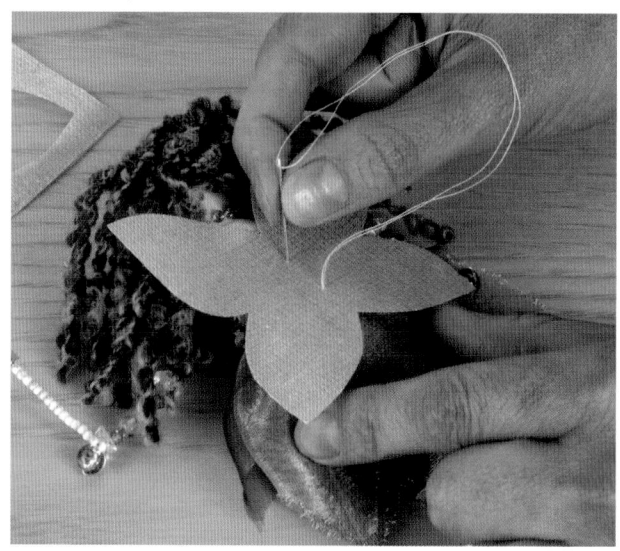

11 Sew a row of size 9 turquoise glass rocaille beads around the neck as a necklace. Bring a needle threaded with a single length of thread to the right side of the bodice at the centre of the upper edge. Thread on a 1.2cm (½in) pale pink flower-shaped sequin then an 8mm (5/16in) flower-shaped sequin then a rocaille or cylinder bead. Insert the needle back through the sequins. Pull the thread tight so that the bead sits on the sequins. Repeat to sew a single 6mm (¼in) flower-shaped sequin each side of the centre. Sew sequins to the hair and three 8mm (5/16in) flower-shaped sequins to the blue skirt.

12 Cut two 9cm (3½in) squares of cream organza for the wings. Join the squares together with fusible webbing. Use the template on page 125 to cut out the wings. Sew the wings to the back of the fairy with a large stitch at the centre. Fold the wings in half to crease them and then open them out flat again.

festive fairy

Make a pretty Christmas fairy to adorn a Christmas tree. Use gold and cream organza for the bodice and skirt and pale yellow stranded embroidery cotton (floss) for the hair. Gold and crystal beads and star-shaped sequins add a festive touch. Insert a 30cm (12in) length of wire into the body through the slipstitched lower edge. The extending end of the wire can be wrapped around the tree.

daisy-chain necklace

Whether you're on the beach, at a picnic or a party, this fresh floral multi-strand necklace says it all.

Three strands of beaded daisies, graduating in length, are suspended between three-hole end bars. The beading technique is easy to master – any size of round bead is suitable for the daisies as long as they are all the same size.

Choose pretty jewellery findings to complement the summery feel of the design. The better the quality of the findings, the more exclusive the necklace will look.

the magic ingredients...

2g of size 9 pale pink pearlised rocaille beads

8g of size 9 turquoise satin rocaille beads

2g of size 9 mauve satin beads

3 beads to use as stop beads

pink Nymo thread

size 10 beading needle

6 silver calotte crimps

8 x 4mm (5/16in) silver jump rings

instant-bonding glue

snipe-nose (flat-nose) pliers

2 silver three-hole end bars

silver torpedo necklace clasp

1 Thread a beading needle with a double 2m (78in) length of thread. Attach a stop bead to the end (see page 22), leaving a 25cm (10in) trailing thread end. Slip on 12 pale pink pearlised beads.

2 To form one daisy, thread on four turquoise satin beads. These satin beads will form the 'petals' of the flower.

3 Thread on a mauve satin bead for the daisy centre. Insert the needle back through the first turquoise bead, as shown above, taking the thread through the bead toward the stop bead.

4 Thread on two turquoise beads and take the needle through the fourth turquoise bead in the direction shown in the photograph. Pull the thread so that the turquoise beads form a neat circle around the mauve bead.

words of wisdom...

If you wish, the beads in between the daisies can be a different size.

5 Thread on a pale pink bead. Repeat step 2–5 to make a row of 55 daisies with a pale pink bead between each daisy. Thread on 12 pale pink beads at the end to complete the first strand of the necklace.

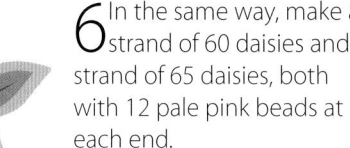

6 In the same way, make a strand of 60 daisies and a strand of 65 daisies, both with 12 pale pink beads at each end.

words of wisdom...

If you want to make the drape between each strand larger, simply make the second and third strands longer.

7 Insert the thread at the end of a necklace through the hole in a calotte crimp. Tie the thread in a large knot and cut off the excess thread. Glue the knot in one cup of the calotte crimp with instant-bonding glue.

8 Carefully squeeze the cups closed with a pair of snipe-nose pliers. Slip the loop of the calotte crimp onto a jump ring and close the jump ring with the pliers. Fix the end of the remaining strands to calotte crimps and jump rings in the same way. Remove the stop beads and fix the start of the strands to calotte crimps and jump rings.

words of wisdom...

It is important to open jump rings sideways; do not pull the jump ring open outwards as it will weaken and may not go back into a perfect circle. Ideally use two pairs of pliers for this job – it gives you more control than trying to work with one set of pliers and the fingers and thumb of your free hand.

9 Lay the strands in a row in order of length. Fix the jump rings to the holes of a three-hole end bar (see page 15).

10 Fix the end bars to a torpedo necklace clasp with a jump ring. Secure the jump rings with a dot of instant-bonding glue at the joins.

flower-fairy bracelet

Make a dainty bracelet with a single strand of daisies. Here,
the petals are worked with size 7 green glass rocaille beads,
the centres are gold and the beads between the daisies are
silver-lined clear glass. The bracelet fastens with a lobster
claw clasp and jump ring.

acorn evening bag

Woodland motifs of acorns and oak leaves adorn this elegant silk evening bag, which measures a dainty 16.5 x 16cm (6½ x 6¼in) – perfect for a fairy princess off to a ball. Lining and wadding provide extra body and protect the beaded stitching, and there's a surprise inside – a pretty charm attached next to the fabric-covered press studs that form the closure.

This bag is easy to make and can be decorated in all sorts of ways – see the alternatives on page 87. In fact, once you make your first one you may feel compelled to make more!

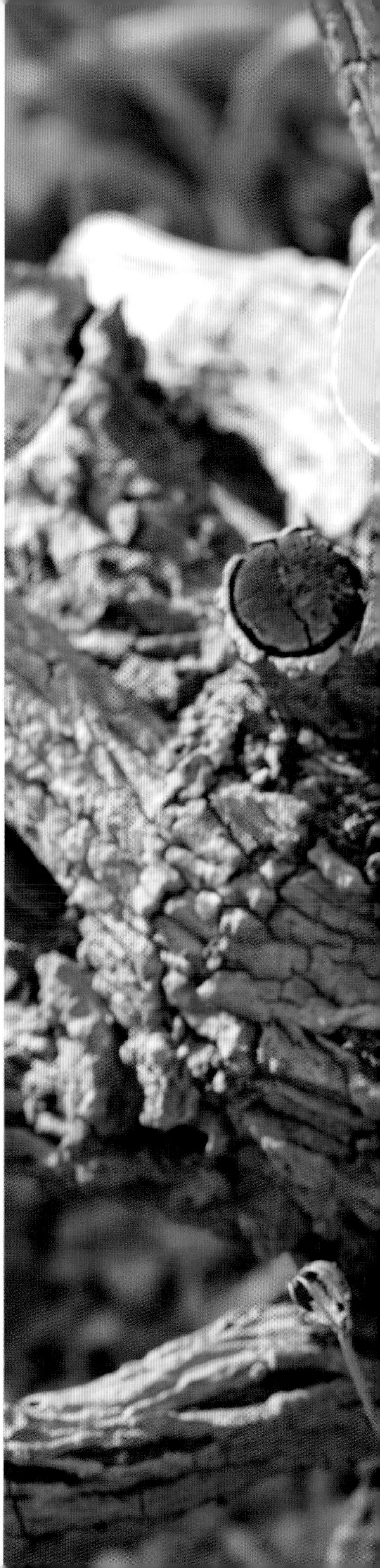

the magic ingredients...

5g of size 11 gold rocaille beads

5g of size 11 copper cylindrical beads

1 x 6mm (¼in) beige glass bead

3 x 2cm (¾in) cranberry flat oval beads

3 x 1.2cm (½in) beige frosted glass bugle beads

1 gold charm – acorns are idea

40cm (½yd) of 90cm (36in) wide white silk dupion

33 x 19cm (13 x 7½in) rectangle of white lining

38 x 19cm (15 x 7½in) rectangle of 50g (2oz) wadding

34 x 1.5cm (13¼ x ⅝in) strip of medium-weight sew-in interfacing

air-erasable fabric marker pen

size 10 crewel embroidery needle

white sewing thread

1.5cm (⅝in) press-stud

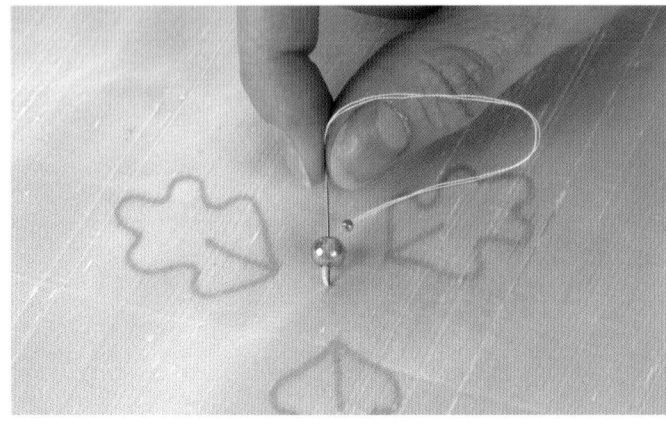

1 Cut a 38 x 19cm (15 x 7½in) rectangle of silk dupion. Using the template on page 124, draw the oak leaves on the right side of the rectangle 5.5cm (2¼in) below the short upper edge of the silk using an air-erasable fabric marker pen. Bring a needle threaded with a double length of thread to the right side at the dot. Thread on a 6mm (¼in) beige glass bead and a size 11 gold rocaille. Insert the needle back through the beige glass bead and fabric.

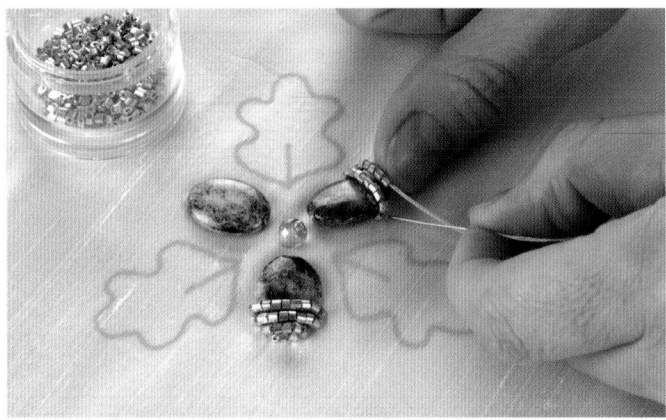

2 Sew a 2cm (¾in) cranberry flat oval bead between each drawn leaf for the acorns. Bring the needle out at one side of one bead about a third down from the outer end of the bead. Thread on enough copper cylindrical beads to wrap over the oval bead. Insert the needle at the other side of the bead. Add three more rows of beads to cover the top of the oval bead. Repeat to make a 'cap' for each acorn.

3 Sew size 11 gold rocailles along the outline of the oak leaves less than a bead's width apart. Sew a bugle bead along the centre of each leaf.

4 Pin and tack the wadding to the wrong side of the silk rectangle. Fold the silk in half with right sides facing and short edges matching. Stitch the side edges, taking a 1.5cm (⁵/₈in) seam allowance. Carefully trim away the excess wadding in the seam allowance. Press the seams open using a silk setting on your iron.

5 Match the fold at the bottom of the bag to the lower edge of one seam. Pin and stitch across the seam at right angles 2.5cm (1in) from the end of the seam, as shown. Repeat on the other side seam. Trim the seam allowances to 5mm (¼in).

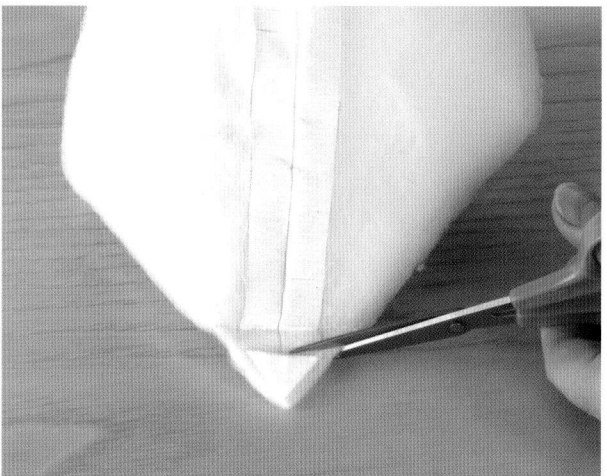

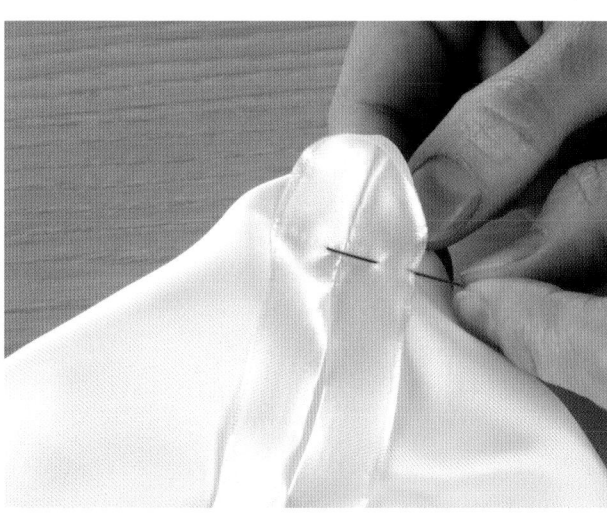

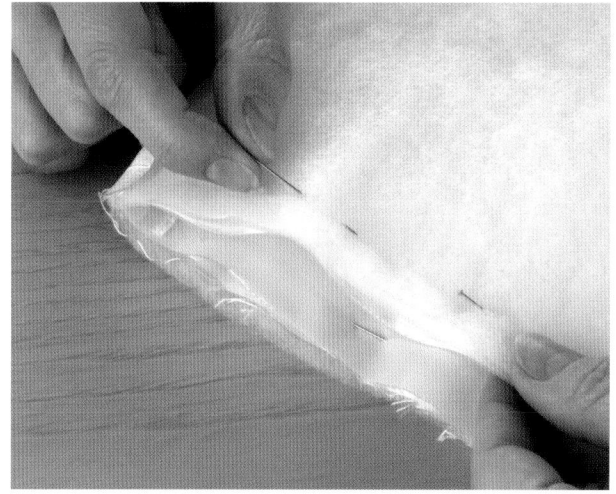

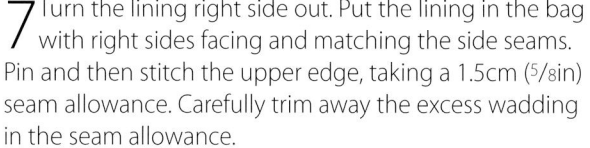

6 Fold the lining in half with right sides facing and short edges matching. Stitch the two side edges, taking a 1.5cm (⁵/₈in) seam allowance and leaving a 13cm (5in) gap in one seam. Press the seams open. Stitch the bottom corners as explained in step 5.

7 Turn the lining right side out. Put the lining in the bag with right sides facing and matching the side seams. Pin and then stitch the upper edge, taking a 1.5cm (⁵/₈in) seam allowance. Carefully trim away the excess wadding in the seam allowance.

8 Turn the bag right side out through the gap in the lining. Slipstitch the gap closed. Push the lining into the bag. Press the top of the bag to the inside for 1cm (³/₈in).

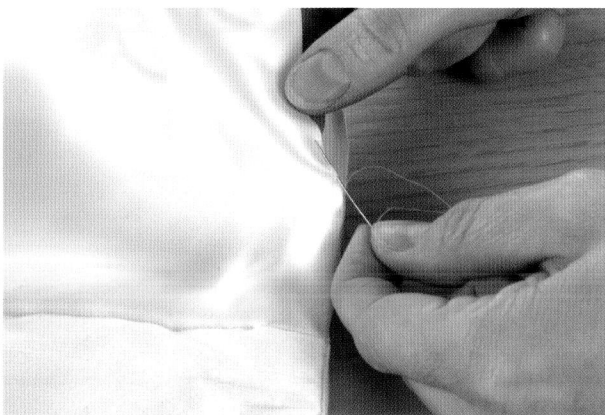

9 Cut a 36 x 6cm (14¼ x 2³/₈in) bias strip of silk for the handle. Press under 1cm (³/₈in) on one long edge. Place the interfacing strip on the wrong side of the silk 1.5cm (⁵/₈in) from the long raw edge. Pin the long raw edge and the ends over the interfacing. Pin then slipstitch the pressed edge over the interfacing.

10 Sew copper cylindrical beads 3mm (¹/₈in) below the upper edge of the bag and along both long edges of the handle less than a bead's width apart, sewing through all the layers. Sew the ends of the handle securely inside the top of the bag.

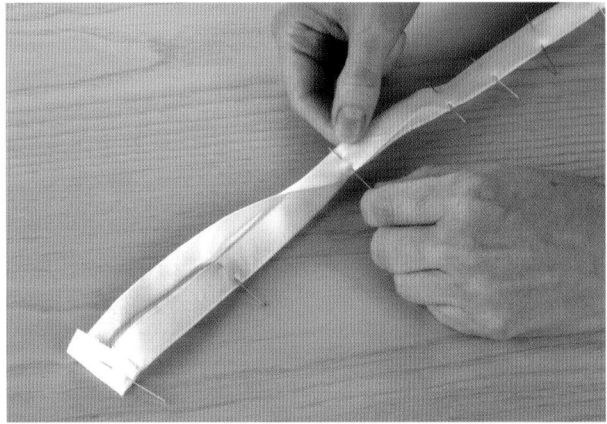

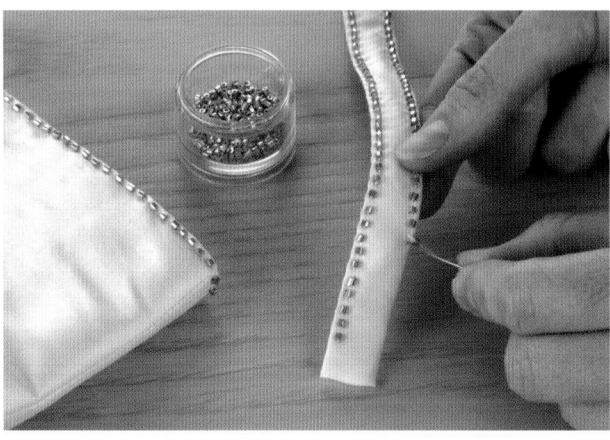

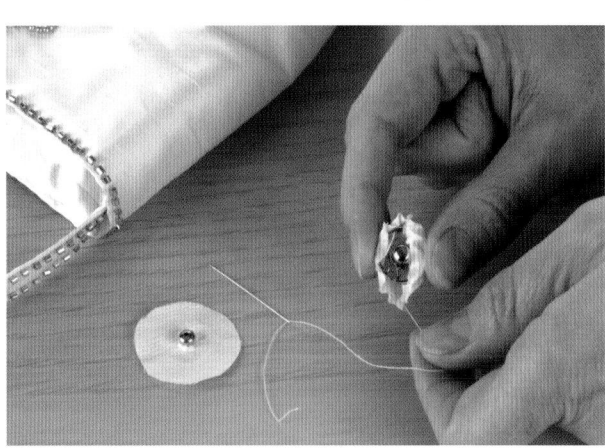

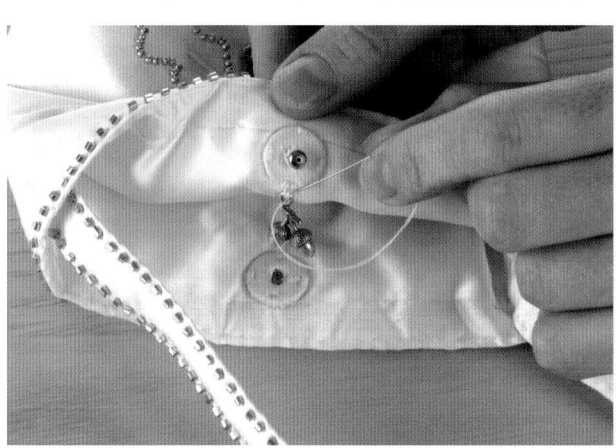

11 To cover the press-stud, cut two 3cm (1¼in) diameter circles of silk. Cut a tiny hole in the centre of one circle. Insert the prong of one section of the press-stud through the hole. Place the other section face down on the wrong side of the other circle. Gather the circumference of the circles and fasten the thread securely on the underside.

12 Sew the press-stud inside the top edge of the bag, sewing through the holes in the metal. Alternatively, you could use a magnetic snap closure, like the ones used by bag manufacturers. These are available from specialist craft stores and bag-making suppliers. Sew a gold charm inside the top edge of the bag for good luck.

A small charm adds a delightful surprise inside the bag.

money and pearls

For the money bag version, metal coins that have a hole punched at the top are used for an unusual border. Just thread on a coin, then a rocaille and then go back through the coin. At the front of the bag add a fringe of varying lengths made from rocaille and bugle beads with a coin on the ends for added flair.

For the pearl fringing shown on the second bag, first attach a border of small pearls around the top edge using backstitch. Add the bead dangles between every three beads, threading down to the bottom and then back up to the top of each string.

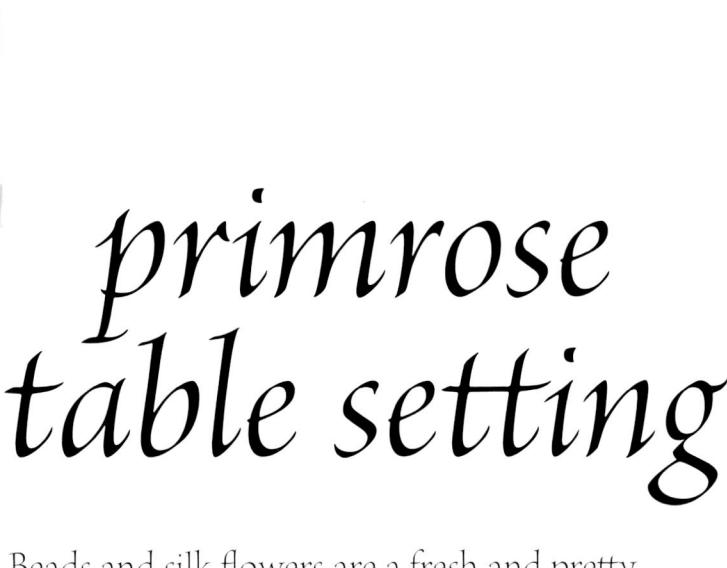

primrose table setting

Beads and silk flowers are a fresh and pretty combination ideal for weddings, Christenings and other special occasions. Here, lovely silk primulas, flower-shaped sequins, pearls and small beads are combined with wire and easy-to-use polymer clay to make a delightful table setting for a summer wedding.

The beads and sequins here have been chosen to complement the spring colours of the flowers. If the wedding has a colour theme, make sure it is also the dominant colour of your flowers and beads.

the magic ingredients...

about 14 x 4mm (1/8in) white pearls

about 10 purple Delica beads

2g of green Delica beads

about 9 size 11 lilac rocaille beads

about 11 assorted 6–8mm (1/4–5/16in) glass and plastic beads

pack of 1cm (3/8in) flower-shaped sequins

mother-of-pearl butterfly

about 12 x 2cm (3/4in) diameter artificial flowers

23cm (9in) of 0.9mm silver wire

reel of 0.315mm silver wire

light green polymer clay (see the tip, below)

thick yellow handmade paper

round-nose pliers

wire snips

baking parchment

instant-bonding glue

thick needle

words of wisdom...

Blend bright green and white polymer clay together to create a lighter shade of green.

1 Roll a 3cm (1¼in) diameter ball of light green polymer clay for the base of the place name. Flatten the clay to about 1.5cm (5/8in) thick on a piece of baking parchment.

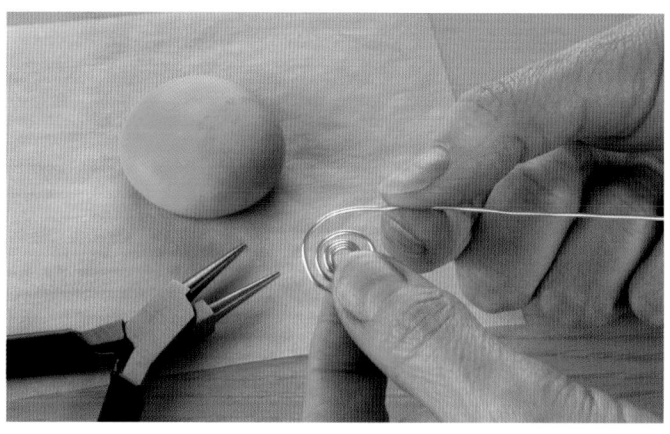

2 Use a pair of round-nose pliers to coil the end of a 23cm (9in) length of 0.9mm silver wire. Keep turning the wire in your fingers, leaving 8cm (3 1/8in) of the wire straight. Insert the wire upright in the centre of the clay.

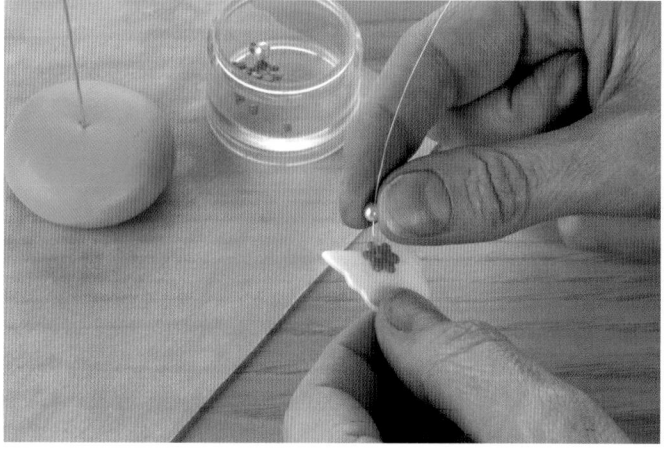

3 Insert a 20cm (8in) length of 0.315mm silver wire through the hole at the top of the mother-of-pearl butterfly. Adjust the butterfly to the centre of the wire and bend down the wires each side of the butterfly. On each end of the wire, thread a flower-shaped sequin, a white pearl and enough purple Delica beads to reach the bottom of the butterfly. Twist the wires together under the butterfly then insert the wire into the clay.

4 Remove the flower heads from about ten silk flowers. Thread a pearl onto the centre of a 20cm (8in) length of 0.315mm silver wire. Twist the wires together once under the pearl. Thread on a flower head. Now thread a green Delica bead onto one wire only.

5 Twist the wires together for 1.5cm (⅝in). To make a leaf, thread green Delicas onto one wire for 2.5cm (1in). Bend the beaded wire into a ring and twist both wires together to the end. Make about seven flowers with beaded leaves. Refer to step 4–5 to fix about three flower heads and seven flower-shaped sequins on 15cm (6in) lengths of wire, omitting the leaves and using lilac rocaille beads instead of pearls on the sequins.

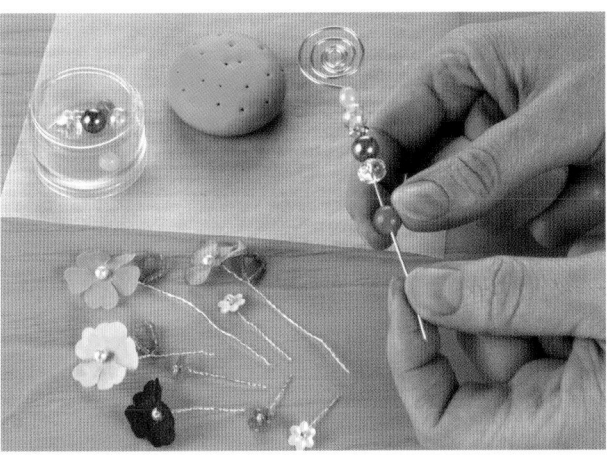
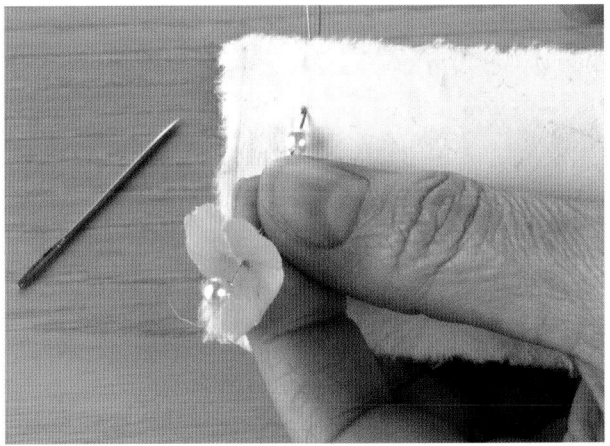

6 Push the ends of the wires into the clay around the coiled wire and butterfly. Snip some wire stems shorter to make a pleasing display. Remove all the wires and bake the clay following the manufacturer's instructions. Leave to cool. Thread about 11 assorted 6–8mm (¼–⁵⁄₁₆in) glass and plastic beads onto the straight end of the coiled wire, leaving 1.5cm (⅝in) at the end of the wire free of beads. Dab instant-bonding glue on the ends of all the wires and insert them into the holes on the clay.

8 Pierce a hole on each side of the flower and insert one wire to the right side through each hole. Thread on a pearl, a flower-shaped sequin and a lilac rocaille bead. Insert the wire back through the sequin, pearl and hole on the place-name card. Twist the wires together on the back and snip off the excess wire. Don't forget to add the name to the card.

7 Tear an 8 x 4.5cm (3¼ x 1¾in) rectangle of handmade paper for the place-name card. Pierce a hole 1.2cm (½in) in from the left-hand corner of the place name with a thick needle. Thread a pearl onto the centre of a 20cm (8in) length of 0.315mm silver wire. Insert the wire ends through a flower head followed by another pearl, then pass the ends through the hole in the place-name card.

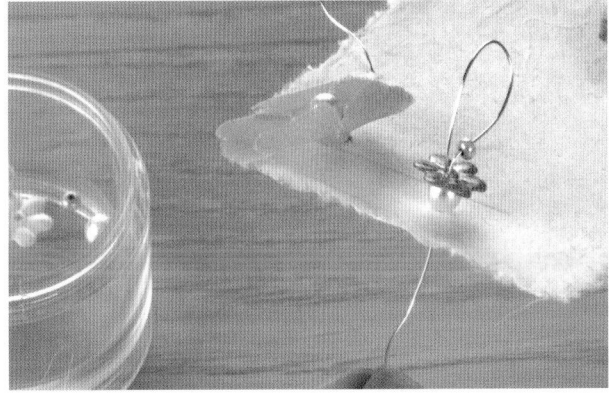

exotic flower brooch

This highly original brooch can be made as flamboyant or dainty as you wish depending on the beads you choose and the number of elements that you add. At its heart is a beautiful crystal, caught in place by wire wrapping – a simple technique that is useful for attaching stones that haven't been drilled with a hole. Use the colour combination shown here or choose your own favourites – or those of the recipient if this is to be a gift.

Semi-precious stones and crystals are said to have meanings. Choose a stone for the centre of the brooch that says something to the wearer: quartz to amplify energy, jade to draw true love closer or fluorite to bring order out of chaos.

the magic ingredients...

10g metallic purple/gold Delica beads

20 x 4mm (1/8in) apricot freshwater pearl beads

24 x 4mm (1/8in) cream pearl beads

10 assorted pearl and glass beads

4 x 4mm (1/8in) translucent grey beads

2 rock crystal chips

1 crystal or semi-precious nugget for the centre of the brooch

scrap of white fabric

1.5cm (5/8in) metal perforated disc, available from craft and jewellery-making suppliers

1.5cm (5/8in) brooch back

beading needle and sewing thread

large-eyed needle

gold knitting wire, such as 0.315mm wire

wire snips

instant-bonding glue

1 Cut a 3cm (1¼in) circle of white fabric. Work a small running stitch around the circle close to the edge. Place the perforated disc face down on the centre of the circle and pull up the gathers tightly. Fasten the thread securely. Pierce the outer holes of the perforated disc through the silk with a large-eyed needle. The holes will close up as you work so re-pierce them when necessary.

2 Thread five Delica beads up to the centre of a 45cm (18in) length of knitting wire. Thread the left-hand end of the wire through the last bead on the right-hand end of the wire, forming a circle, as shown.

3 Thread two Delica beads onto the right-hand end of the wire. Thread one Delica bead onto the left-hand end of the wire. Thread the left-hand end of the wire through the last bead on the right-hand end of the wire, towards the ring of beads. Repeat until the beaded strip is 7.5cm (3in) long.

4 Insert each end of the wire through a bead at the other end of the beaded strip. To form a 'petal', insert both ends of the wire through one outer hole on the disc front. Wrap the wire around the outer edge of the disc and insert the wires through the hole again.

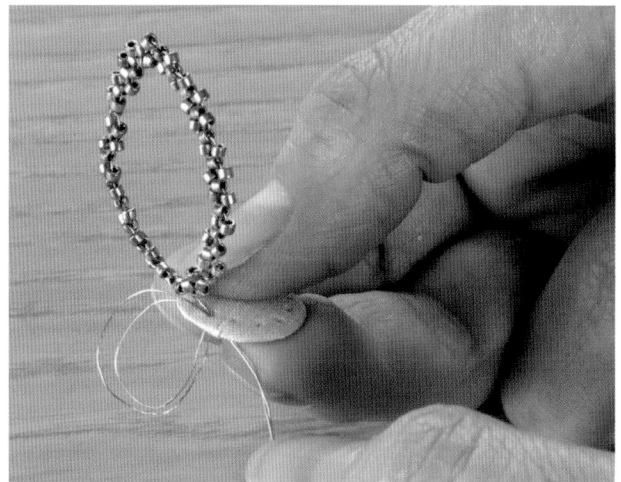

5 Take one end of the wire and thread on six 4mm (1/8in) apricot pearls. Insert the wire back through all the pearls except the last one.

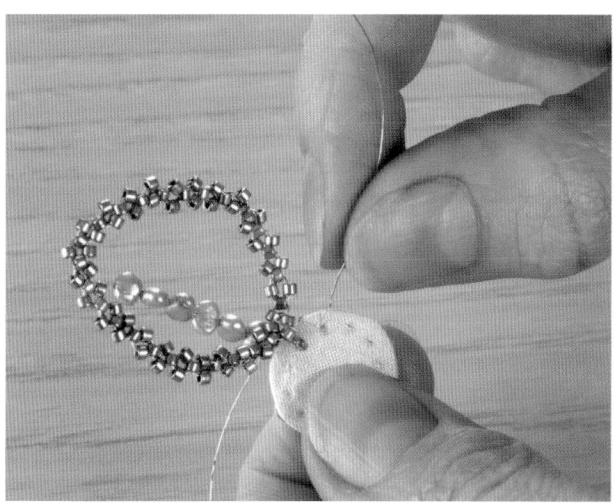

6 Insert the wire through the same hole on the disc front. Pull the wire so that the pearls sit next to each other neatly within the petal. Wrap the wire around the outer edge of the disc and insert the wire through the hole again. Bring the other wire to the right side through the next pierced hole.

7 Thread on a large bead and a smaller pearl bead. Insert the wire back through the large bead. Insert the wire through the hole on the disc back. Pull the wire so that the base of the bead is against the disc. Wrap the wire around the outer edge of the disc and insert the wire through the hole again. Repeat steps 2–7 twice more, spacing the beads and petals evenly.

8 Twist all the wires together for 1cm (3/8in) on the underside of the disc. Snip off the excess wire and press the twisted wires to the centre of the disc.

9 Thread a 4mm (1/8in) translucent grey bead onto the centre of a 25cm (10in) length of wire. Insert both ends of the wire through 22 x 4mm (1/8in) cream pearls. Insert the wires through a pierced hole. Wrap the wires around the outer edge of the disc and insert the wires through the hole again.

10 Thread a Delica bead up to the centre of a 35cm (14in) length of wire. Insert both ends of the wire through a large bead. Thread a 4mm (1/8in) bead or pearl onto one end of the wire.

11 Twist the wires together for 1.2cm (½in). Thread a bead, chip or pearl on one wire. Repeat three times then twist the wires together for 1.2cm (½in). Make two more wired lengths of beads. Insert the wires through a pierced hole. Wrap the wire around the outer edge of the disc and insert the wire through the hole again. Twist all the wires together for 1cm (3/8in) on the underside of the disc. Snip off the excess wire and press the twisted wires to the centre of the disc. Dab the twisted wires with instant-bonding glue.

12 Snip two 50cm (19in) lengths of wire. Insert both wires from the back, bringing them out through a pierced hole; take them back through a hole on the opposite side of the disc. Slip the crystal under the wires. Pull the wires tight. Repeat to hold the crystal securely in place, inserting the wires through the holes of a brooch back as you work and wrapping them around the outside of the disc. Twist all the wires together for 1cm (3/8in) on the underside of the disc. Snip off the excess wire. Glue the twisted wires to the brooch back with instant-bonding glue to finish.

words of wisdom...
If the perforated disc has prongs on the sides, trim them off with wire snips.

fairy wand

This pretty wand is made in the same
way as the brooch using pale pink, green,
silver and crystal beads but it has three
extra strands as described in step 9 for the
brooch. The beaded decoration is bound
and glued to the top of a garden stick that
has been painted silver. The wand is not
suitable for young children but would look
lovely hanging on a wall.

leaf-vine belt

This delicately beaded silk belt is garlanded with a leaf vine of tiny metallic beads and edged with sequins and silver beads for a truly romantic look. The belt, which can be made in three sizes, sits on the hips – perfect with a flowing skirt – but you could easily adapt it to fit your waist using straight pieces of fabric and interfacing. The belt fastens with rouleau ties embellished with additional sequins and beads.

The gold and silver colours of this belt enhance its glamorous look, but these are easily altered to suit a favourite outfit. What about a combination of blue and silver or black and gold, for example?

the magic ingredients...

10g of silver Delica beads

10g of gold/purple Delica beads

5g of gold 4mm (1/8in) sequins

5g of transparent fawn 4mm (1/8in) sequins

60cm (3/4yd) of 90cm (36in) wide pale gold silk dupion

30cm (1/2yd) of 90cm (36in) wide pelmet interfacing

matching sewing thread

size 10 embroidery needle

gold stranded cotton embroidery cotton

water-erasable fabric marker pen

bodkin

1 Refer to the template on page 123 to cut two belts on the fold from silk dupion and one from pelmet interfacing. Pin and tack the interfacing centrally to the wrong side of a silk belt. Draw the vine with the fabric marker pen on the right side of the silk fabric.

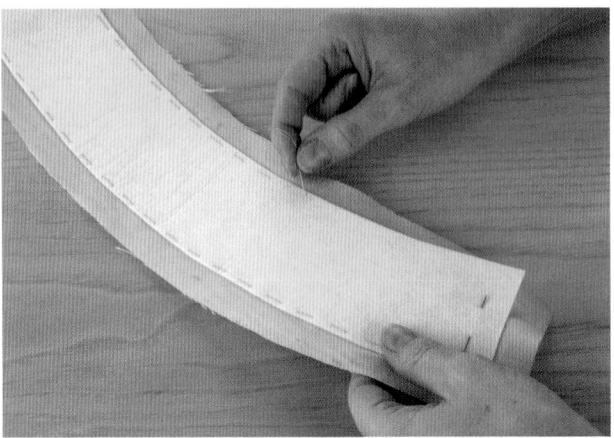

2 Sew silver Delica beads along the stem 1mm (1/24in) apart. Sew gold/purple Delica beads along the outline of the leaves 1mm (1/24in) apart.

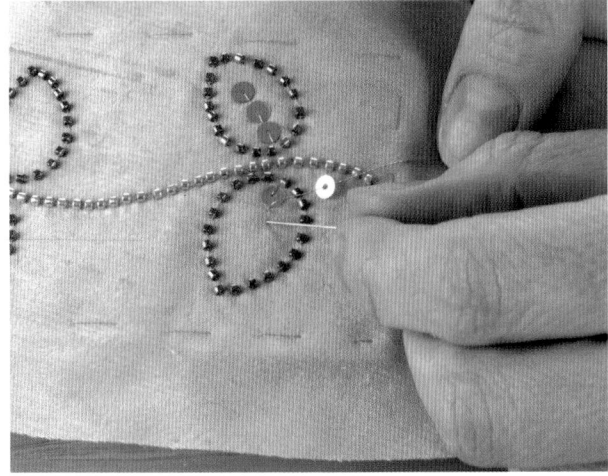

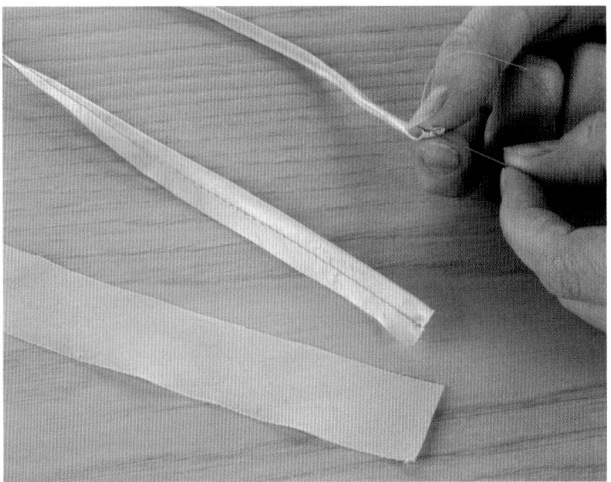

3 Sew three gold sequins along the centre of each leaf using a single strand of gold stranded embroidery cotton, as shown here.

4 Cut six 35 x 2.5cm (14 x 1in) bias strips of gold silk dupion for the ties. Fold the ties lengthways in half with right sides facing. Stitch the long edges, taking a 5mm (1/4in) seam allowance. Turn right side out using a bodkin then turn in one end of each tie and slipstitch closed.

5 Pin and Tack the raw ends of three ties centrally to each end of the beaded belt, as shown here.

6 Lay the silk fabric pieces together with right sides facing then tack in place. Machine stitch all round the interfacing, leaving a gap at the centre of the lower edge. Clip the seam allowance across the corners. Trim one seam allowance to 6mm (¼in) and the other to 4mm (⅛in). Turn the belt right side out and remove the tacking. Slipstitch the opening closed. Press the belt.

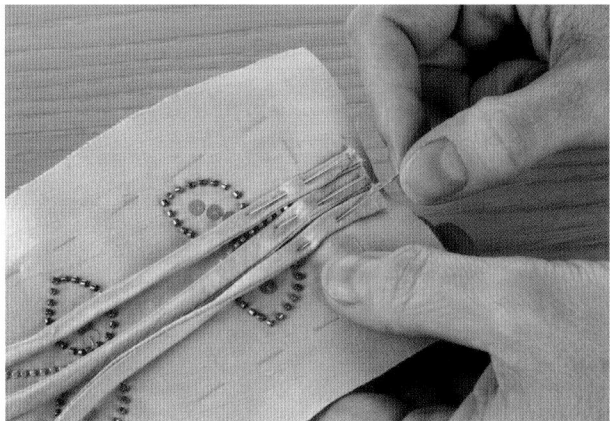

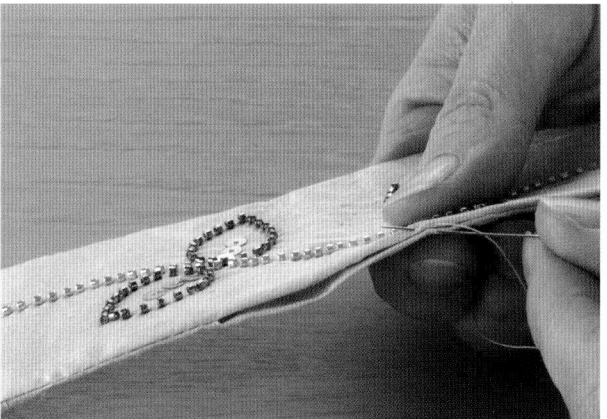

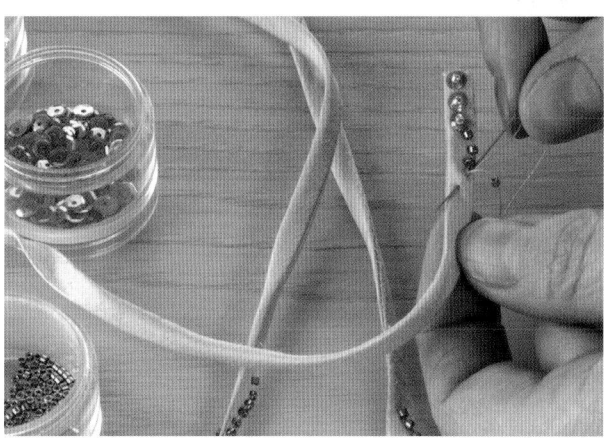

7 Sew transparent fawn 4mm (⅛in) sequins 8mm (5/16in) apart just inside the edges of the belt. Start by bringing the needle up through the fabric then thread on a sequin and a silver Delica bead. Insert the needle back through the sequin and top layer of fabric. Pull the thread so that the bead sits on the centre of the sequin and continue along the edges of the belt.

8 To decorate the ties, sew three transparent fawn 4mm (⅛in) sequins each topped with a silver Delica bead to the free end of each tie. Sew gold/purple Delica beads in a curved line from the last sequin 1mm (1/24in) apart. Repeat on the other side of the tie.

clematis ring
and bracelet

The star-shaped petals of the clematis flower inspired

this delightful ring and coordinating bracelet. Clever

but simple beading techniques form the petals using

sapphire-coloured bicone crystals but like the real

flower, your creation can bloom in whatever hue(s)

you fancy.

*There are plenty of crystal and
crystal-imitation beads available but
Swarovski crystals, like the ones used
here, are particularly fine and will add
a luxurious look to your jewellery.*

the magic ingredients...

for the ring:

5g size 11 blue rocaille beads

bicone crystals:
20 x 3mm (1/8in) sapphire blue
11 x 4mm (1/8in) sapphire blue
5 x 5mm (3/16in) sapphire blue

80cm (32in) silver-coloured knitting wire, such as 0.315mm wire

instant-bonding glue

wire snips

1 Thread five rocaille beads up to the centre of a 45cm (18in) length of knitting wire. Thread the left-hand end of the wire through the last bead on the right-hand end of the wire, as shown, forming a circle.

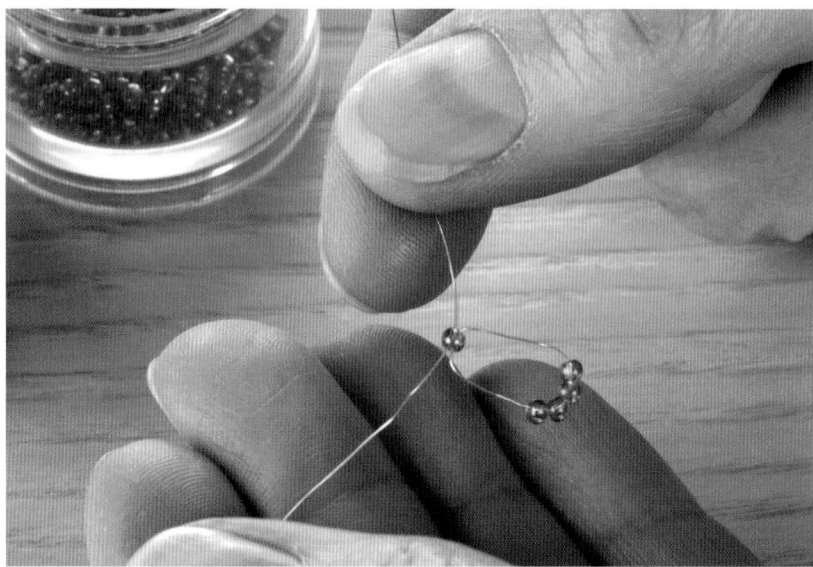

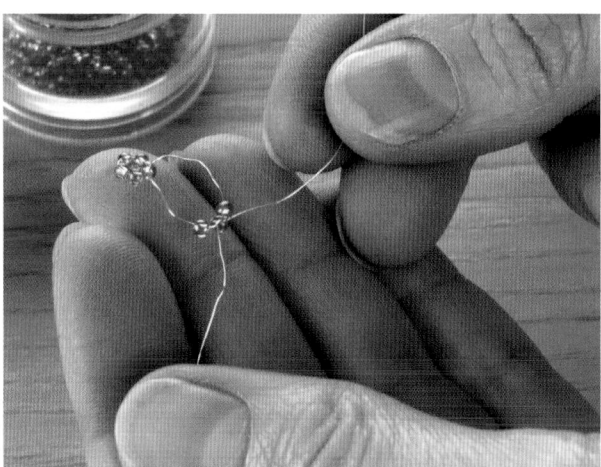

2 Thread two rocailles onto the right-hand end of the wire. Thread one rocaille bead onto the left-hand end of the wire. Thread the left-hand end of the wire through the last bead on the right-hand end of the wire, towards the ring of beads. Repeat until the beaded strip is long enough to wrap around your finger and meet end to end. (See also steps 2 and 3 on page 94 for this technique.)

3 Insert each end of the wire through a bead at the opposite end of the beaded strip. Twist the wire ends together and dab the twists with instant-bonding glue. Weave the wires through the ring and snip off the excess.

4 To make the flower, thread three 3mm (1/8in) crystals onto the centre of a 35cm (14in) length of knitting wire. Insert both ends of the wire through a 3mm (1/8in) crystal.

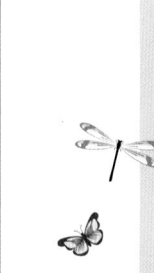

words of wisdom...

You can add depth to your ring by using two shades of crystals in the flower, one at the centre and the other around the edges. (The central beads are 5mm or 3/16in.)

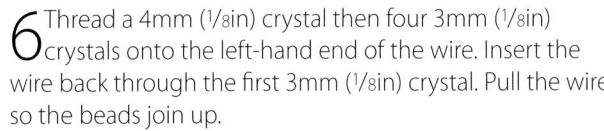

5 Thread a 4mm (¹/₈in) crystal then a 5mm (³/₁₆in) crystal onto each end of the wire. Insert the right-hand end of the wire through the left-hand 5mm (³/₁₆in) crystal to form the first petal, as shown.

6 Thread a 4mm (¹/₈in) crystal then four 3mm (¹/₈in) crystals onto the left-hand end of the wire. Insert the wire back through the first 3mm (¹/₈in) crystal. Pull the wire so the beads join up.

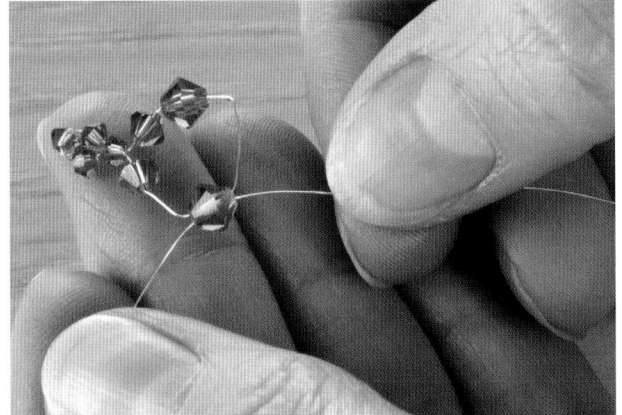

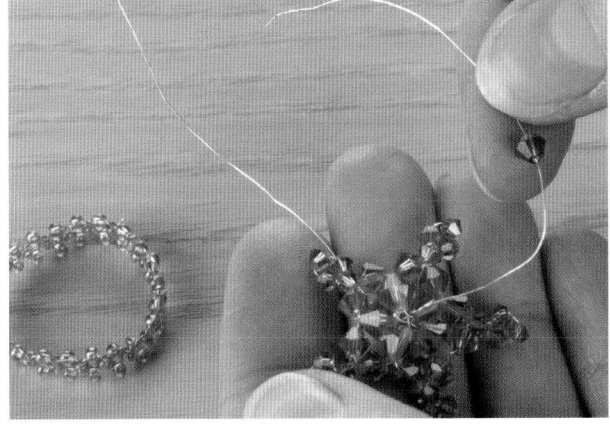

7 Thread a 4mm (¹/₈in) crystal then a 5mm (³/₁₆in) crystal onto the left-hand end of the wire. Insert the other end of the wire through the last 5mm (³/₁₆in) crystal.

8 Repeat steps 6 to 7 twice. Repeat step 6. Thread on a 4mm (¹/₈in) crystal. Insert the wire through the first 5mm (³/₁₆in) crystal. Twist the wires together at the centre on the underside. Bring one wire to the front and thread on a 4mm (¹/₈in) crystal. Take the wire back to the underside and twist the wires together again. Weave the wires through the beads on the ring. Stick the underside of the centre of the flower to the ring with instant-bonding glue. Snip off the excess wire with wire snips.

matching bracelet

Make a matching bracelet by weaving a 1.5cm (⁵/₈in) wide band of rocaille beads on a bead loom as explained on pages 24–26, and fasten the bracelet with an 8mm (¼in) bicone crystal and loop (see page 26). Follow step 4–8, above, to make a large flower for the bracelet using a 45cm (18in) length of wire and replacing the 3mm (¹/₈in) crystals with 4mm (¹/₈in) crystals, the 4mm (¹/₈in) crystals with 5mm (³/₁₆in) crystals and the 5mm (³/₁₆in) crystals with 6mm (¼in) crystals.

winged trinket box

Sumptuous and elegant, the lovely blue beaded wing design on this box is worked with rocaille beads in backstitch on silk fabric. The rim of the lid is finished with a beaded polka-dot design woven on a bead loom and the overall effect is simply stunning. You'll want to save this box for your most prized treasures or use it as a gift box for a really special friend.

This box is lined with toning printed paper. If you intend to use it as a gift box, you could nestle the gift in downy feathers for protection, continuing the wing theme.

the magic ingredients...

10g of blue glass size 9 rocaille beads

8g of silver size 9 rocaille beads

5g of clear glass size 9 rocaille beads

45cm (½yd) of 90cm (36in) wide lilac silk dupion

10cm (4in) of 90cm (36in) wide blue silk dupion

18 x 13.5cm (7 x 5⅜in) oval papier mâché box, 7cm (2¾in) deep

20cm (8in) square of 115g (4oz) wadding

50cm (20in) of 1.2cm (½in) wide mauve satin ribbon

co-ordinating printed paper or giftwrap

22cm (8½in) embroidery hoop

bead loom

blue Nymo thread

size 10 beading needle

size 10 embroidery needle

tracing paper

sharp HB pencil

1.2cm (½in) and 2cm (¾in) wide double-sided tape

spray adhesive

1 Using a sharp pencil, transfer the template for the wings on page 125 onto a piece of lilac silk dupion that is at least 2cm (¾in) larger all round than the top of the lid. Stretch the fabric in the embroidery hoop. Bead the design lines using a single length of Nymo thread and a size 10 embroidery needle. Work in backstitch, catching a blue rocaille bead with every stitch, as shown.

2 Cut an oval of wadding to fit the lid. Stick this to the top of the lid with pieces of 2cm (¾in) wide double-sided tape. Cut a 5cm (2in) wide bias strip of lilac silk dupion that is the length of the circumference of the lid plus 2.5cm (1in). Apply 2cm (¾in) wide double-sided tape around the outside and inside of the rim. Stick the upper edge of the bias strip to the lower half of the outside of the rim, folding under the raw end of the overlap. Stick the other edge inside the lid.

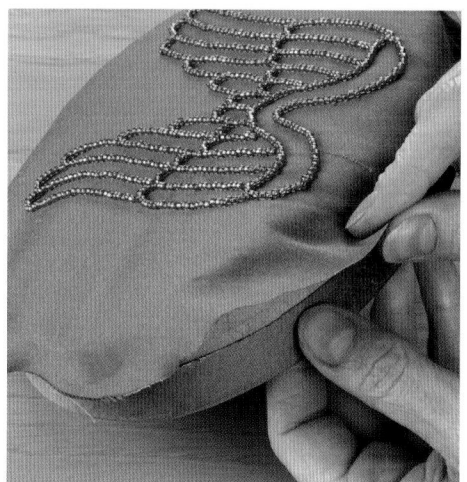

3 If you haven't already done so, trim the beaded wings fabric to the same size as the lid with a 2cm (¾in) margin added all round. Place the beading centrally on the lid. Smooth the fabric outwards from the centre and stick the edges onto double-sided tape on the lid rim.

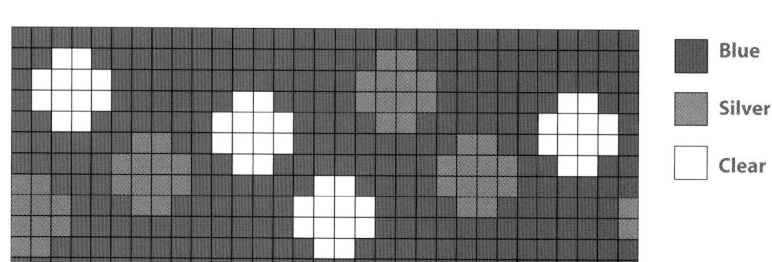

	Blue
	Silver
	Clear

4 Follow the chart below left to weave a band of 13 warp threads using blue glass, clear glass and silver metal rocaille beads. Refer to the instructions on pages 24–26 as needed. Repeat the design until the band is long enough to wrap around the rim of the lid and meet edge to edge. Weave all the thread ends into the weaving, leaving one thread free to join the ends of the weaving together.

words of wisdom...

The most time-consuming element of this project is the loom-woven lid band. If desired, simply attach ribbon to the rim lid to cover the raw edges and replace with braid.

5 Apply 2cm (¾in) wide double-sided tape around the outside of the box rim. Remove the tape backing and stick the beaded band around the rim. Slipstitch the ends together neatly with the remaining thread.

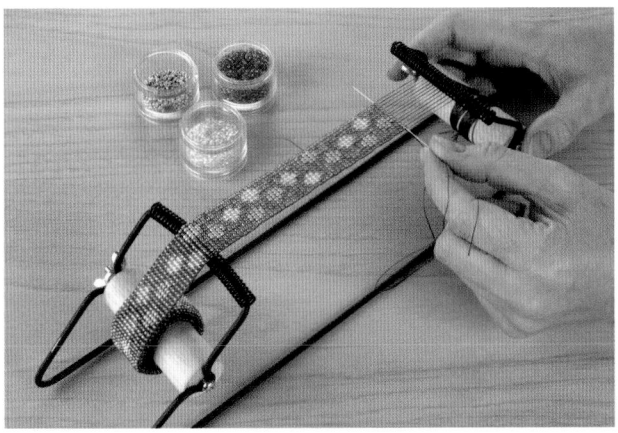

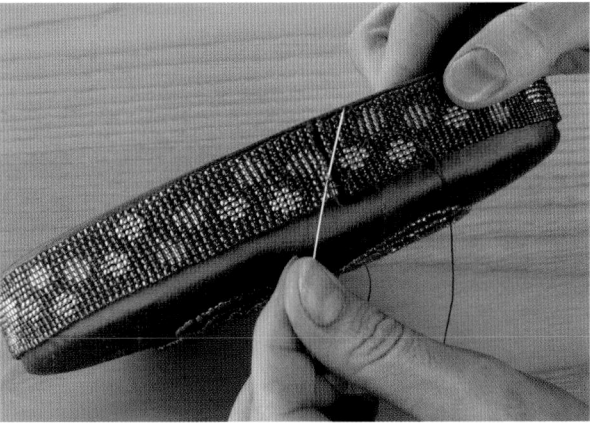

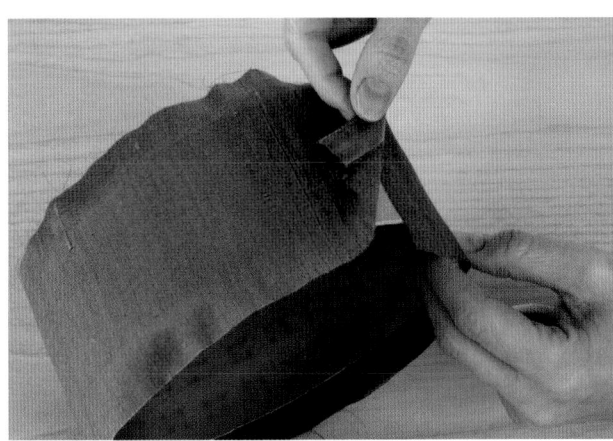

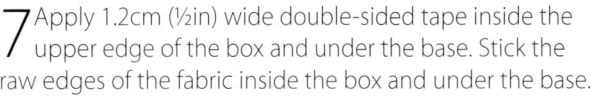

6 Line the box with printed paper or giftwrap using spray adhesive; keep the upper edges level and stick the excess paper onto the base, snipping the paper so that it lays flat. Cut a strip of blue silk dupion 3cm (1¼in) deeper than the depth of the box and long enough to wrap around it plus 2.5cm (1in). Wrap the fabric around the box with the raw edges extending equally above and below the box and fold under the raw end of the overlap. Stick the overlap in place with 1.2cm (½in) wide double-sided tape, as shown.

7 Apply 1.2cm (½in) wide double-sided tape inside the upper edge of the box and under the base. Stick the raw edges of the fabric inside the box and under the base.

8 Apply 1.2cm (½in) wide double-sided tape over the raw fabric edge inside the box. Stick 1.2cm (½in) wide mauve satin ribbon over the raw edge, as shown. Stick the overlap in place with more double-sided tape. Cut ovals of printed paper or giftwrap to line the underside of the lid and both sides of the box base. Stick these in place with spray adhesive to finish.

berry pendant
and earrings

Winter berries are the inspiration for this lovely jewellery. Delicate organza ribbon suspends a pendant of luscious 'berries' made from fabulous cranberry-coloured freshwater pearls. You'll want earrings to match, and these are made in the same way but using fewer pearls. The whole set is quick and easy to make.

Freshwater pearls are available in many lovely colours, some elegantly subtle, others gloriously rich. The cranberry pearls are wonderful for winter but you could make a set for every season.

the magic ingredients...

33 x 6mm (½in) cranberry-coloured potato-shaped freshwater pearls

33 x 3.8cm (1½in) silver headpins

27 x 4mm (⅛in) silver jump rings

12cm (5in) of 0.24 gauge wire

2 silver calotte crimps

necklace clasp (S-hook and ring)

60cm (24in) of 6mm (¼in) wide cranberry-coloured organza ribbon

wire snips

round-nose pliers

snipe-nose (flat-nose) pliers

instant-bonding glue

words of wisdom...
If you can't find a matching ribbon, use a coloured cord, leather thong or silver chain instead.

1 Thread a pearl onto a headpin. With a pair of wire snips, snip off the excess wire, leaving 8mm (⁵/₁₆in) above the pearl.

2 Hold the headpin with a pair of round-nose pliers 3mm (⅛in) from the tips. Bend the wire towards you to form a loop centred over the pearl. Repeat with all the pearls and headpins. You will need 15 pearls for the pendant and 9 pearls for each earring.

3 Slip the loop of a pearl onto a 4mm (⅛in) jump ring. Close the ring with both pairs of pliers. This pearl will be at the bottom of the pendant.

4 Slip another jump ring onto the first jump ring. Hang a pearl on each side of the first jump ring. Close the ring with both pairs of pliers as before.

5 Add six more jump rings with a pearl at each side to form the necklace pendant. Fix a jump ring between the pearls on the last jump ring and slip the organza ribbon through it.

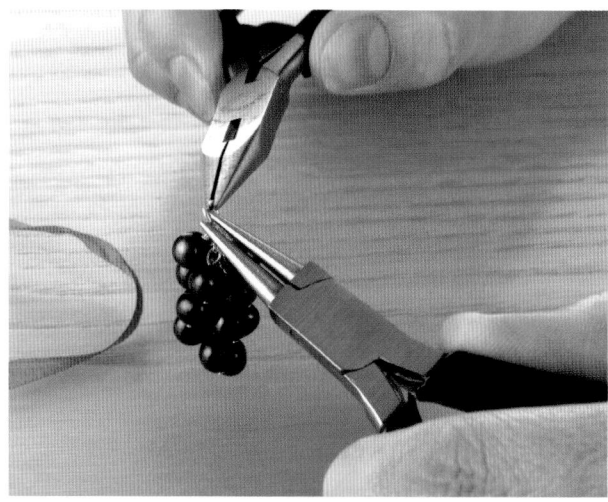

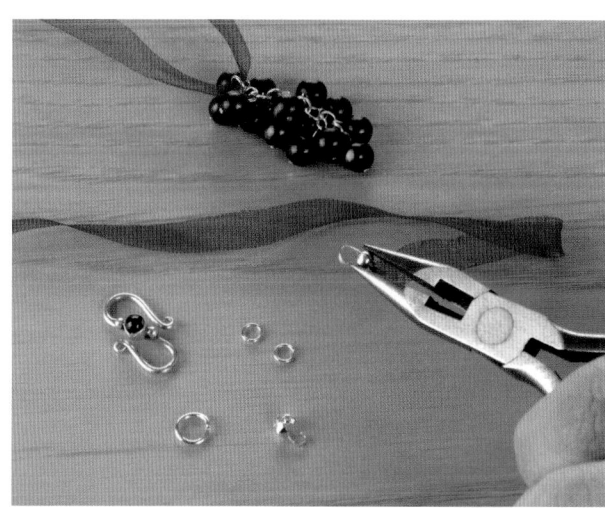

6 Thread a 12cm (5in) length of 0.24-gauge wire through one end of the ribbon. Bend the wire in half and twist the wire ends together – this will enable you to thread the ribbon through the calotte crimp. Thread the wire 'needle' through the hole in a calotte crimp. Cut off the needle and tie a knot at the end of the ribbon. Cut off the excess ribbon close to the knot.

7 Rest the knot in the cup of the calotte crimp. Dab with Instant-bonding glue to secure in place. Close the cup with a pair of snipe-nose pliers. Repeat at the other end of the ribbon. Fix a jump ring to each calotte crimp then join a necklace clasp to the jump rings.

8 To make each earring, first follow step 3–4. Add six more jump rings with a pearl at each side to form each earring pendant. Fix a jump ring between the pearls on the last jump ring. Slip an earring wire onto the last jump ring and close the fitting.

words of wisdom...
Dab the joins of the jump rings with instant-bonding glue for added security.

113

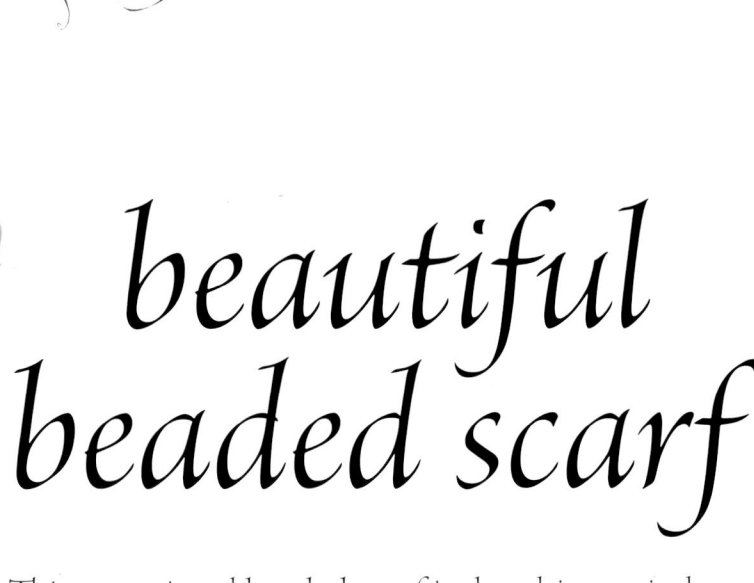

beautiful beaded scarf

This sensational beaded scarf is the ultimate in luxury either for yourself or a lucky friend. Both ends are embellished with stylized flowers, clusters of beads and sequins and a lovely netted edging of lilac cylinder beads, pearls and silver rocailles. These beads won't cost the earth but they will look absolutely stunning on a scarf suitable for a very special occasion.

This scarf is made from crepe fabric. You can substitute any luxury fabric from silk to fine wool.

the magic ingredients...

22 x 4mm (1/8in) dark red drop beads

12 x 8mm (5/16in) pale blue freshwater pearls

52 x 4mm (1/8in) apricot freshwater pearls

18 x 6mm (1/4in) apricot freshwater pearls

324 white Delica beads

144 size 11 silver rocaille beads

12 x 1.2cm (1/2in) blue leaf-shaped beads

22 x 3mm (1/8in) pale blue beads

5g of 2mm (1/16in) lilac cylinder beads

16 transparent shell-shaped sequins

40cm (16in) of 120cm (48in) wide dusky pink crepe fabric

dressmaking pins

size 10 embroidery needle and beading needle

dusky pink sewing thread

1 Mark lengthways along the centre of the scarf with a row of dressmaking pins. Mark the position of two flowers on one end of the scarf with pins at least 6cm (2½in) in from the raw edges and centre line. With a double length of sewing thread, attach a 4mm (1/8in) dark red drop bead at one flower position. Stitch three 8mm (5/16in) pale blue freshwater pearls around the drop bead.

2 Bring the needle to the right side between two pearls. Thread on 18 white Delicas. Insert the needle back through the fabric next to where the needle emerged, forming a loop. Bring the needle to the right side inside the top of the loop and insert it the other side of the loop to hold the loop in place and form a petal. Repeat between the other pearls.

words of wisdom...

You can buy 'dress' scarves made from fairly fine folded fabric, which are an ideal base for this project. If the scarf already has fringing you can omit the beaded edging. Make sure you stitch through one layer of fabric only.

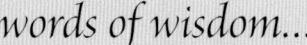

3 Bring the needle to the right side 5mm (¼in) from one pearl. Thread on a 4mm (⅛in) apricot freshwater pearl and a size 11 silver rocaille. Insert the needle back through the apricot pearl. Repeat at the end of each pale blue pearl. Now bring the needle to the right side between a beaded petal and a pale blue pearl. Thread on a blue leaf bead and a size 11 silver rocaille. Insert the needle back through the leaf bead. Repeat to add two more leaves. Bead a flower at the other flower position.

4 Mark the position of three bead clusters among the flowers. Sew a 3mm (⅛in) pale blue bead at one position. Sew three 6mm (¼in) apricot freshwater pearls around the pale blue bead. Bring the needle to the right side between two pearls. Thread on a 4mm (⅛in) apricot freshwater pearl and a size 11 silver rocaille. Insert the needle back through the small apricot pearl and fabric. Repeat between the other pearls.

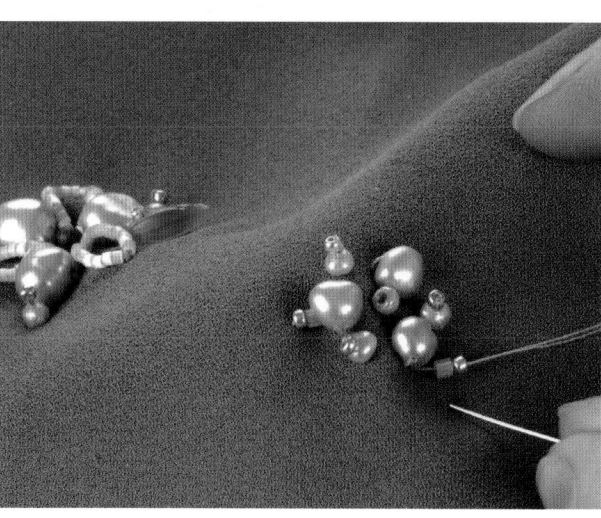

5 Bring the needle to the right side at the end of a large apricot pearl. Sew on a 2mm (¹⁄₁₆in) lilac cylinder bead and a silver rocaille bead. Repeat to add a cylinder and silver rocaille bead at the end of each large pearl. Sew bead clusters at the other positions. Repeat at the other end of the scarf.

6 Plan the positions of eight pairs of shell sequins along the scarf. Bring the needle up in position and thread on two sequins and a silver rocaille bead. Insert the needle back through the sequin and bring it out through another hole in both sequins. Thread on a silver rocaille bead, insert the needle back through the sequins and fabric. Repeat to attach the other pairs of shells. Remove the centre line pins. Fold the scarf lengthways in half with right sides facing. Stitch the long and short edges taking a 6mm (¼in) seam allowance and leaving a gap to turn right side out. Clip the corners and turn the scarf to the right side. Slipstitch the opening closed and press the scarf.

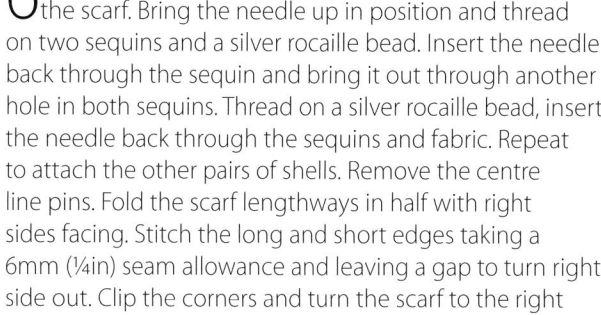

7 Mark one end of the scarf with dressmaking pins at 2.5cm (1in) intervals. Thread a beading needle with a long double length of pink thread. Secure the thread to one corner of the scarf. To make the first row of netting, thread on a 4mm ($\frac{1}{8}$in) apricot freshwater pearl, a silver rocaille bead, six lilac cylinder beads, a silver rocaille bead, a 3mm ($\frac{1}{8}$in) pale blue bead, a silver rocaille bead, 6 lilac cylinder beads, a silver rocaille bead and a 4mm ($\frac{1}{8}$in) apricot freshwater pearl for the first loop. Make a small stitch in the edge of the fabric at the first pin mark. Insert the needle back through the apricot pearl and silver rocaille bead.

8 Thread on the same sequence of beads and attach loop by loop to make eight loops. At the end of the row, insert the needle through the apricot pearl and silver rocaille bead. Thread on eight lilac cylinder beads, a silver rocaille bead, three white Delicas, a dark red drop bead and three white Delicas. Insert the needle through the silver bead toward the start of the first row and thread on six lilac cylinder beads.

9 Insert the needle through the three beads at the centre of the first row. Continue working the second row, but threading on three lilac cylinder beads except on the last half of the last loop where eight lilac cylinder beads should be threaded on. Insert the needle through the silver rocaille bead and apricot pearl at the start of the first row then secure the thread in the fabric. Repeat at the other end of the scarf.

The netted edge on this scarf adds a lovely, delicate touch. Detailed instructions on netting can be found on page 21.

an enchanting collection

charm bracelet, page 30

fairy-ring cushion, page 34

blackberry candleholder, page 50

napkin ring, page 55

magical greetings, page 56

festive fairy, page 75

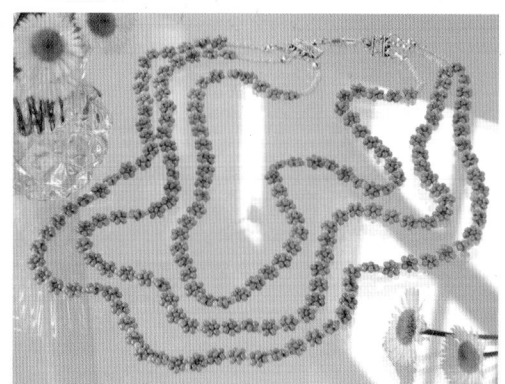

daisy-chain necklace, page 76

flower bracelet, page 81

fairy wand, page 97

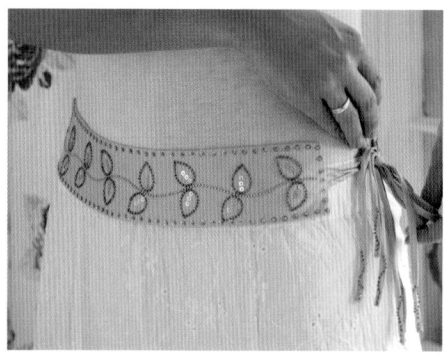

leaf-vine belt, page 98

clematis ring and bracelet pages 102–5

christmas snowflakes, page 40

tooth-fairy box, page 44

lavender bag, page 49

beautiful beaded butterflies, page 60

toadstool charms, page 64

fairy princess, page 70

acorn evening bag, page 82

evening bags, page 87

primrose table setting, page 88

exotic flower brooch, page 92

winged box, page 106

berry pendant and earrings, page 110

beautiful beaded scarf, page 114

templates

Here are the templates needed for the projects in this book. They are all full size except the leaf-vine belt, opposite, which should be enlarged on a photocopier by 200%. Alternatively, scan the template into a computer and enlarge as desired. Once the template is the correct size you will need to transfer it to fabric. There are various ways of doing this but two simple options are described below.

transferring a template with a pencil

If the fabric is finely woven fabric and pale, trace the template onto tracing paper with a sharp HB pencil. Turn the tracing over and redraw it on the wrong side. Tape the tracing right side up on the fabric with masking tape. Redraw the design to transfer it.

using dressmaker's carbon paper

If the fabric is dark, trace the template on tracing paper with a sharp HB pencil. Tape the tracing right side up on the fabric with masking tape. Slip dressmaker's carbon paper under the tracing, coloured side down and redraw the design to transfer it.

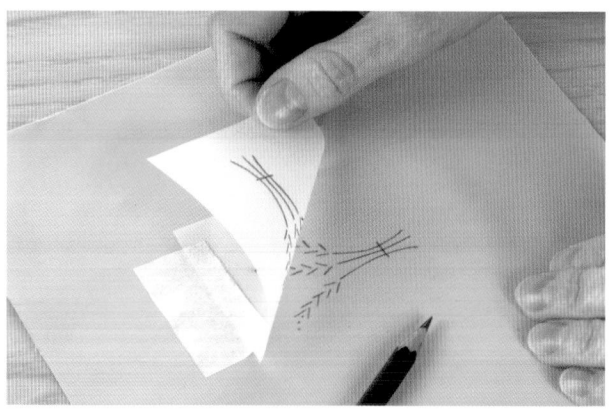

words of wisdom...

If your fabric is pale and fairly thin, you can transfer a design using a light box or window with the light behind it. Simply tape the template or a tracing of it on the glass, fix your fabric on top using masking tape and then trace the design lines directly.

The pattern for this design was transferred using the method above left. See page 49 for this project.

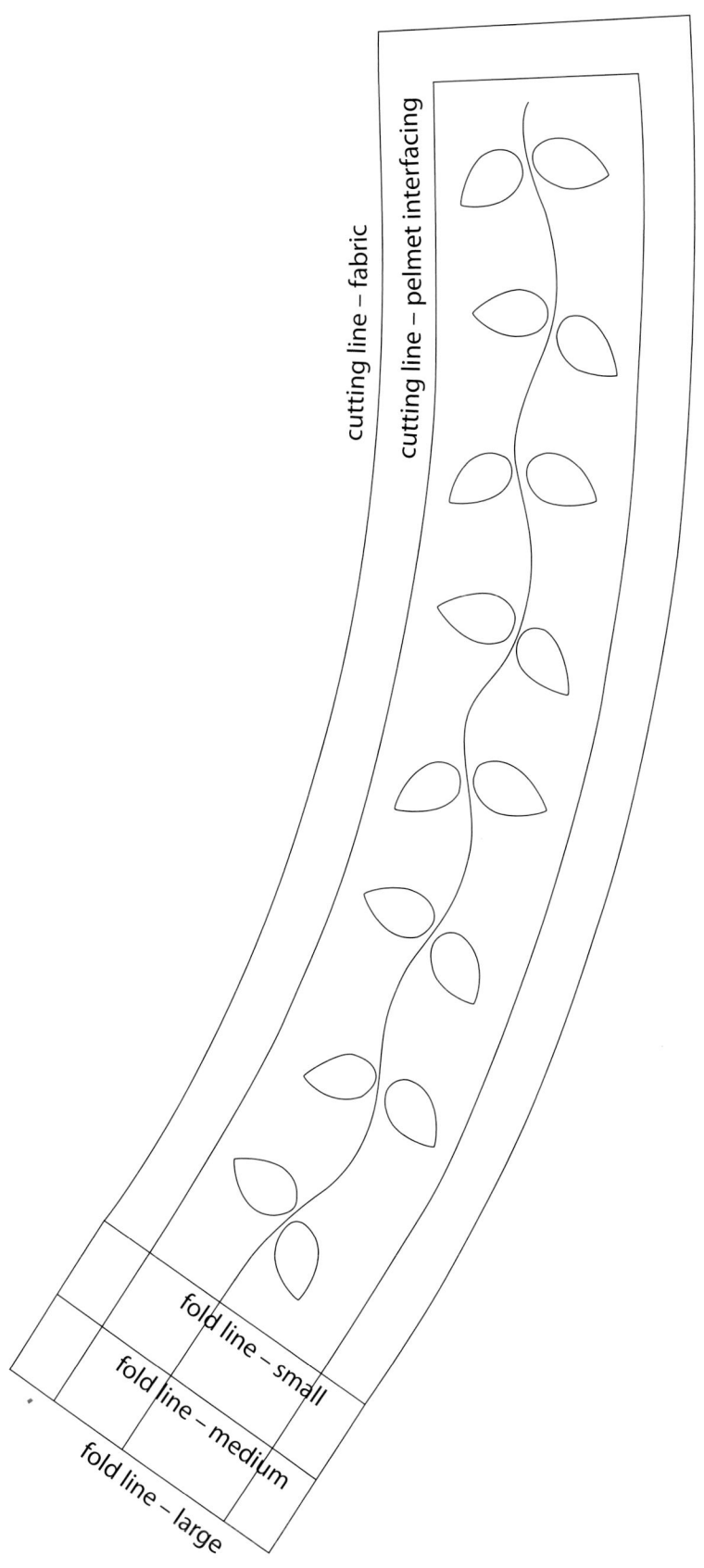

leaf-vine belt
(*see page 98*)

Enlarge this pattern
by 200%

cutting line – fabric

cutting line – pelmet interfacing

fold line – small

fold line – medium

fold line – large

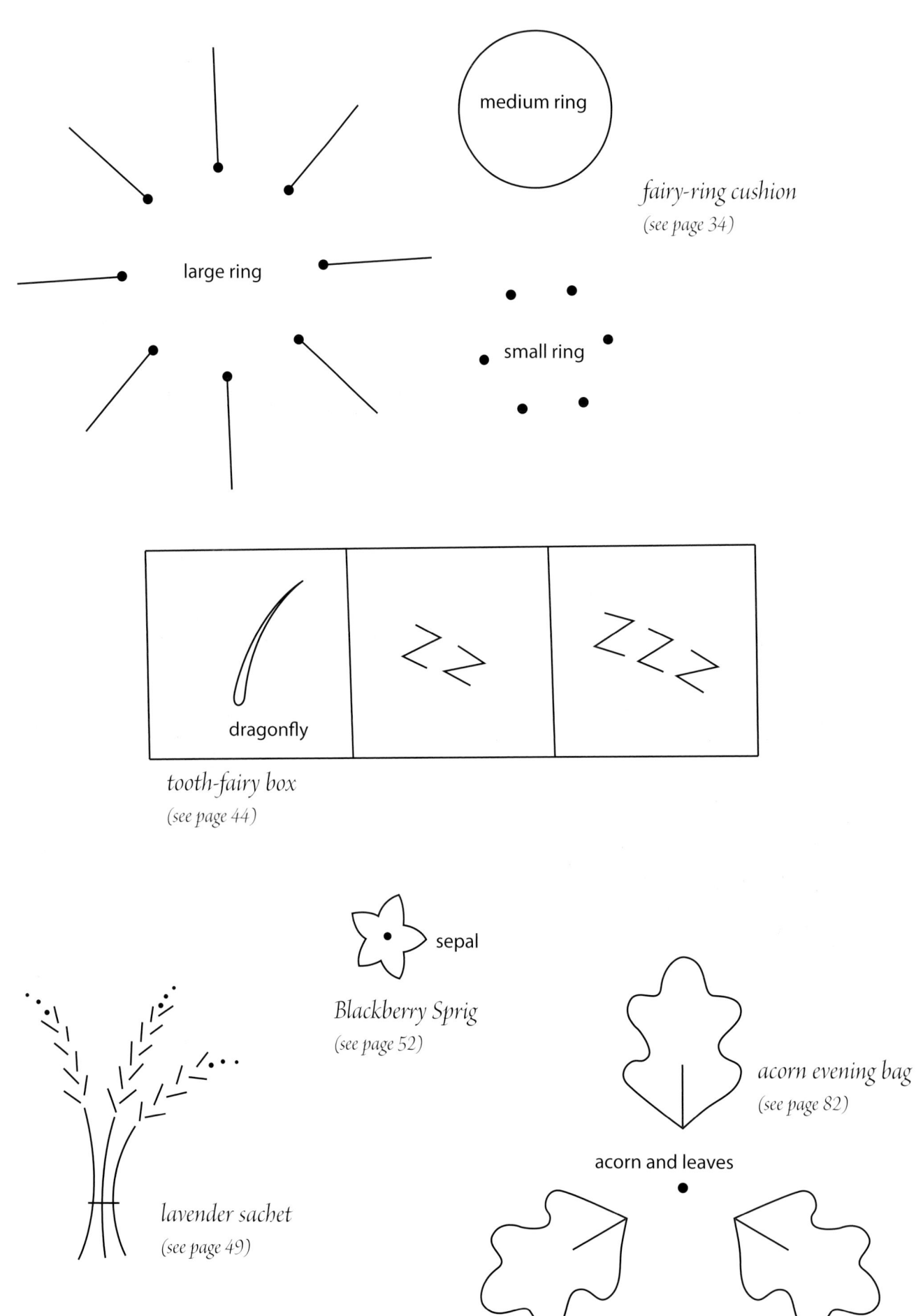

medium ring

fairy-ring cushion
(see page 34)

large ring

small ring

dragonfly

tooth-fairy box
(see page 44)

sepal

Blackberry Sprig
(see page 52)

acorn evening bag
(see page 82)

acorn and leaves

lavender sachet
(see page 49)

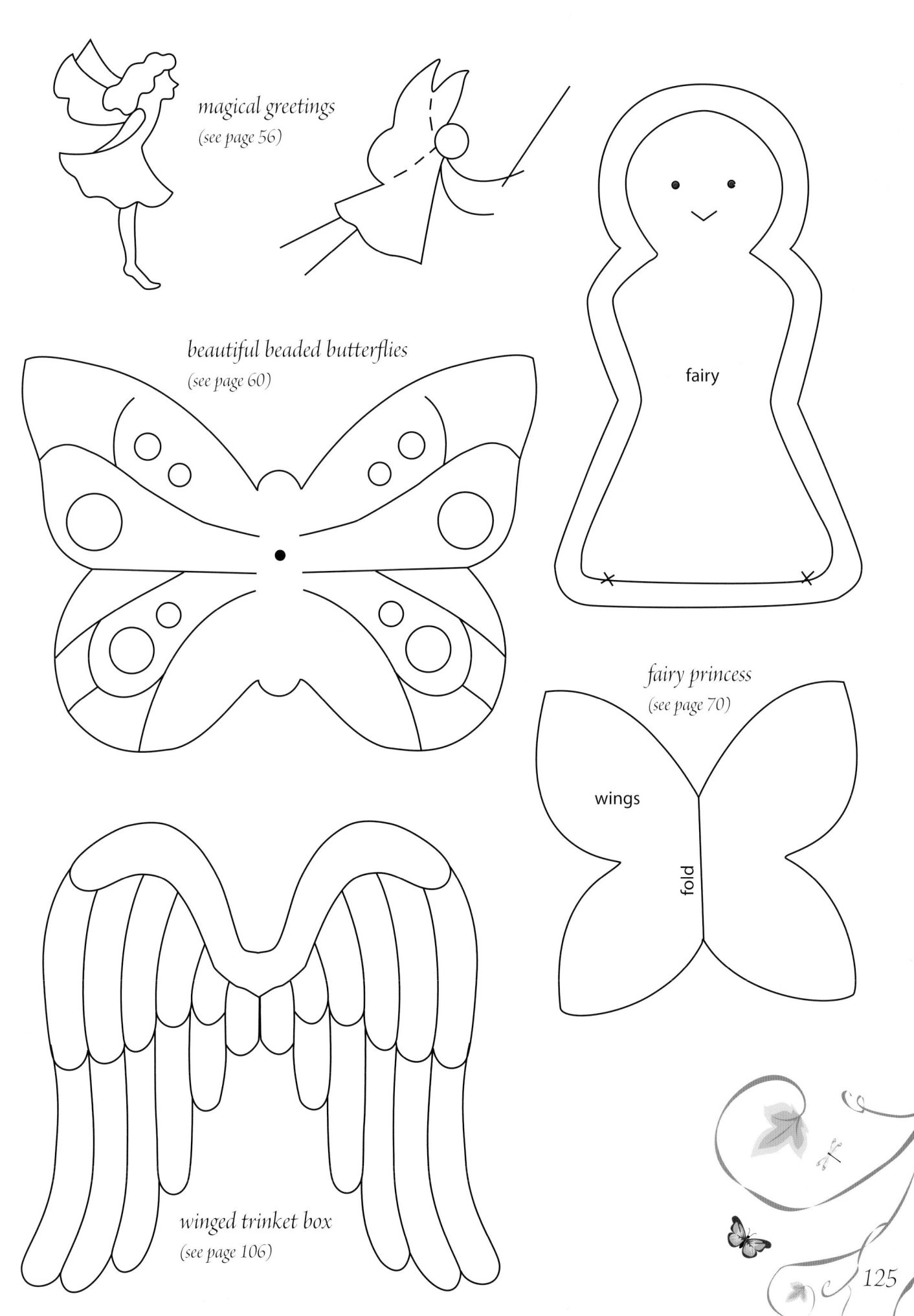

magical greetings
(see page 56)

beautiful beaded butterflies
(see page 60)

fairy

fairy princess
(see page 70)

wings

fold

winged trinket box
(see page 106)

125

Suppliers

UK

Buffys Beads
2–3 Kingly Court
Carnaby Street
London W1B 5PW
Tel: 0207 494 2323
www.buffysbeads.com
for crystals, dyed mother-of-pearl beads and more

The Bead Shop
21A Tower Street
Covent Garden
London WC2H 9NS
Tel: 020 7240 0931
www.beadshop.co.uk
for a comprehensive selections of beads, tools, findings and advice

Beadworks
21a Tower Street
Covent Garden
London WC2H 9NS
Tel: 0207 240 0931
www.beadworks.co.uk
for jewellery findings, glass beads, charms, rocaille beads and bugle beads

Creative Beadcraft (Ells and Farrier)
20 Beak Street
London W1R 3HA
Tel: 0207 629 9964
www.creativebeadcraft.co.uk
for sequins, crystals, pearls, plastic beads and more

julesgems.com
Unit A, GDS Building
Lancaster Road
Shrewsbury SY1 3LG
Tel: 0845 123 5828
www.julesgems.com
for tools, findings, chains, wire and a huge range of beads

The London Bead Company
339 Kentish Town Road
London NW5 2TJ
Tel: 0870 203 2323
www.londonbeadco.co.uk
for Delicas, rocaille beads and bugle beads

The Silver Corporations
483 Green Lanes
London N13 4BS
Tel: 0845 838 6226
www.thesilvercoporation.co.uk
(also selling internationally via eBay)
for quality beads, findings and accessories including sterling silver and gold-filled

US

All Seed Beads
PO Box 4504
Foster City
CA 94404
www.allseedbeads.com
for many beads ideal for use with a loom

Fire Mountain Gems
One Fire Mountain Way
Grants Pass
OR 97526-2373
Tel: 1-800-423-2319
www.firemountaingems.com
for just about everything to do with beads

Shipwreck Beads
Tel: 1-800-950-4232
www.shipwreckbeads.com
for just about everything including unusual beads, findings, earring clips for non-pierced ears, tools, books and accessories

Silver Rose Beads
9422 Woodland Ave E Puyallup
WA 98371
Tel: 253-845-4949
www.silverrosebeads.com
(also selling internationally via eBay)
specializing in precious and semi-precious beads

The Venetian Bead Shop
Tel: 1-800-439-3551
www.venetianbeadshop.com
good supplier of unusual beads as well as tools, findings and Swarovski crytal beads

about the author

Cheryl Owen is a versatile craft designer. She originally trained and worked in the fashion industry before moving on to apply her flair to various crafts such as beading and papercrafts. She is the author of over forty books and a regular contributor to magazines and partworks.

Index